899

1996 $8.99

Transforming the Daily Grind

Christianity in Practice Series

Transforming the Daily Grind

Life with God Is an Adventure

Stuart Briscoe

Harold Shaw Publishers
Wheaton, Illinois

ISBN 0-87788-504-4

Cover design by David LaPlaca

Library of Congress Cataloging-in-Publication Data

Briscoe, D. Stuart.
    Transforming the daily grind : life with God is an adventure / Stuart Briscoe.
      p.   cm.
    ISBN 0-87788-504-4
    1. Christian life. I. Title.
    BV4501.2.B7424 1994
    248.4—dc20
                                       94-42504
                                       CIP

02 01 00 99 98 97 96 95

10 9 8 7 6 5 4 3 2 1

Contents

1

Are You Sure
You're Alive?

John 11:1-45

Have you ever noticed how much pets physically resemble their owners? It's become a cliché that they look a lot alike, but that's because, like many clichés, this one has a great deal of truth in it.

Not only do pet owners tend to share important physical features with their charges, but they also talk to them and treat them in many ways as though they were human. It's not uncommon to see a person carrying on a conversation with a beloved pet as if the animal were understanding every word and answering back in English! Some people go so far in "humanizing" their pets that they actually take offense if you point out that the pet is in fact an animal, not a human being.

Perhaps if you own a dog, cat, bird, or some other pet, you can identify with these tendencies. But our pets aren't human—they differ from us in significant ways. What are some of the key differences?

Many people say that we are superior to the animals because we are more highly developed. But our superiority over the animals does not stem solely from a more sophisticated development of body and personality. Our superiority is a result of our possessing something in addition to the body and soul that an animal does not possess. This something is called the *spirit.*

The body enables us to be conscious of the physical aspects of life. With the body, we eat, breathe, run, sleep, and see. Our body enables us to walk toward people, to hear what they say, and to shake their hand.

But the body can never enable us to make a friend of that person. It is the soul that enables us to do this, for the soul enables us to understand the person, to respond to him, or to react against him. The soul even gives us the capacity to love the person, and so the soul is that part of us that enables us to have a deeper relationship than a purely physical one. We can enjoy the person we have recognized physically in a social way, too, because we are blessed with a soul.

The spirit is unique in that it gives us a remarkable capacity to know and to enjoy God. It is this ability that makes us superior. The spirit of a human being makes even the lowest person far superior to the highest animal.

A Sense of God

While animals are created beings and undoubtedly have knowledge of God—the Bible says in several places that the created world praises God and even longs for a new heaven and a new earth—the Scriptures don't indicate that animals have spirits that are either alienated from God or in relationship to him. You have never seen a cow standing on its hind legs praying! But strange as it may seem in these days of agnosticism and atheism, every human being has some inherent sense of the reality of God. I believe that no one is born an atheist, and that those who profess to be atheists or agnostics have, at some time, decided to reject those things concerning God that they inherently know in the depth of their being.

It is remarkable that so many who deny the existence of God, such as atheists, or discount or disregard his existence, such as many agnostics, are so enthusiastic in their arguments against him. They appear to take this person, whom they say does not exist, very seriously! One of the reasons they take him so seriously is that they have an inherent consciousness and awareness of his existence.

There never was a human being who did not have a god of some kind. There is something inside a person that makes him long for something or someone bigger than himself for whom he can live, upon whom he can depend, or around which his life can revolve. His god may be an ambition or a hobby, a person, or even himself, but somewhere he will have a god.

We are incapable of functioning without a god. Tribes who live in the most remote corners of the earth have invariably been found to have their own private gods whom they fear, respect, worship, or serve. Every level of society demonstrates ability and capacity to know a god of some kind. Yes, even though some may wish to deny or discount it, we have within ourselves a certain knowledge of God and a certain capacity to know God.

The Signs of Spiritual Life

So far we have seen that people operate on the three planes of body, soul, and spirit. If it is possible for us to operate on three planes, it is also possible that we may not necessarily operate on all three planes simultaneously. For instance, if the body stops operating a person will be physically dead, but that does not automatically mean he will be spiritually dead. Conversely, a body that is going along fine does not mean that the spirit is functioning perfectly. Therefore, it is possible to be physically alive but spiritually dead in one and the same moment. If you are reading this, you are most certainly physically alive. But do not assume that you are necessarily spiritually alive, for it is quite possible that you could be reading this and be dead.

This is not a figment of my imagination. The Bible says, "The widow who lives for pleasure is dead even while she lives (1 Tim. 5:6). Jesus also startled some men by saying, "I have come that they may have life" (John 10:10), but they were already physically alive. So obviously he had not come to give people who were physically alive more physical life.

The lady mentioned by Paul had not died physically. No, she was very much physically alive, but she was spiritually dead. She needed the life that Jesus talked about, and so do we.

Appetite

Would you like to know if you are dead? It is a simple thing to find out. Dead people have no appetite. When a person is alive he gets hungry regularly, but once he dies he loses all interest in food. No matter how appetizing the food may be, or how delicious the aromas that come from the kitchen, he will be totally unmoved.

One of the symptoms of spiritual deadness is lack of appetite for God. That does not automatically imply a lack of appetite for church. Many people get God and church confused. For a number of reasons, it is relatively simple to have an appetite for church without having an appetite for God. Some people have a church appetite because church attendance is a social occasion or because it adds to their prestige. Maybe it makes them feel good to go and they like the music. But God does not enter into their reckoning. No hunger for God means a lack of spiritual appetite, and that usually means spiritual deadness.

The Bible is a bore to many people, although Christ said it is more important than our daily bread. Thousands of people have absolutely no hunger or appetite for the Word of God. They have a copy of it in their home, but they seldom read it. They have no appetite. No appetite can mean no life, and no life always means death. Check on your appetite for God or your lack of it. Check on your hunger for the Word of God.

Activity

When Lazarus in the New Testament was alive, he was an active man. The moment he died, all trace of activity ceased. This is

4

exactly what happens to a person who is spiritually dead. There is a complete absence of spiritual activity. Physical and social activity are common evidences of physical and social life. But a life that is spent working for success, profit, and pleasure, and is never invested in activity on behalf of God's kingdom, is a dead life.

Did you ever hear someone say, "I'm too busy with my profession to get involved in a youth program. I would like to help, but you know how it is—not enough hours in the week!"

This is not unreasonable, because many people are desperately busy. But the same man will make time for golf and bowling, put in a few hours in front of the television set, and never miss a football game. His problem is not too few hours in the week. His problem is that he has no appetite for the sort of activity that is spiritual. We cannot criticize him because of his lack of activity; we can only sympathize, because his lack of activity is a fair indication of his lack of spiritual life. The man is dead.

Awareness

Martha and Mary loved their brother Lazarus, and I am sure their love was returned. When Lazarus died, however, he no longer seemed to be aware of them. Of course not! There is no awareness in a dead man!

Dead men don't love, dead men don't see danger, dead men are unmoved by humor, and pathos doesn't do a thing to them. Dead men are utterly insensitive to what is going on around them.

This lack of awareness and this absence of sensitivity can be translated into the spiritual realm, too. When spiritual realities fail to excite or move people, it is an ominous sign. People can measure things from a physical standpoint and evaluate them from the social point of view, but when they are incapable of evaluating and measuring things on a spiritual basis, it is serious.

Sometimes parents who have ambitions for their children fight their children if they express a desire to be missionaries. "No child of mine is going to bury himself in that God-forsaken hole," they say. "After all I have spent on his education, do you really think I am going to allow this blatant waste of his potential?" These are the words of a person who is no doubt extremely astute, but totally unaware of spiritual realities. This is the language of a dead man!

Lack of appetite, activity, and awareness are symptoms of death, whether it be in the physical or the spiritual realm.

The Need for Spiritual Life

Most people are conscious of a lack in their lives, but they don't know what it is they're lacking. "Something is missing in my life," they say, or "I am looking for something, but I don't know what."

If people are made capable of enjoying spiritual life, but they don't have this spiritual life, it is not surprising that they say something is missing. Many people who admit there is something missing also realize that it is missing in the area of the spirit. Others do not agree, but there is more or less general agreement on the deadness in the center of many lives, even though there is by no means agreement on its cause or its cure.

"People need a good example" cry the well-meaning do-gooders, and they do their best to provide this good example. Men and women who give a good example to their fellow citizens are a tremendous boon to society. But did you ever try to give a dead man a good example? Of course, it is hopeless.

Someone else will come on the scene and say, "Oh, no, he doesn't need an example; he needs encouragement." You know as well as I do that you can be as enthusiastic and encouraging as it is possible to be, but you will never encourage a dead man to be anything but dead.

On the other hand, social workers with an eye on living conditions and the related behavior of some of the less fortunate say, "Change their environment, and all will be well."

"Education will do the trick," others say enthusiastically.

I expect by the time you have tried examples, encouragement, education, and environment, with no response from a dead man, you have grown very discouraged. Many wonderful people have grown utterly disillusioned with the human race. *This is because they have failed to understand that the problem is spiritual.*

If a man is dead, you cannot expect anything from him. If you don't expect anything from him, you will be neither surprised nor disappointed.

All these worthy aids to life will do wonders in certain circumstances, but not one of them or all of them together will do a thing for a dead man. There is only one thing a dead man needs—*life!* If men are spiritually dead, there is only one thing they need—spiritual life.

How to Be Made Spiritually Alive

In the lovely story of the Lord Jesus dealing with Lazarus, we see a perfect illustration of how spiritual life is made available to a person who is spiritually dead.

Jesus Christ himself claimed to be the life that spiritually dead people needed. He started off by explaining that the reason he came into the world was that he might give life, and life "more abundant." He further explained, "I am the Resurrection and the Life."

This Jesus, who is the resurrection and the life, came to the place of Lazarus's burial. He stood outside his tomb and wept. Death in the tomb—and life outside the tomb. What a moment, full of dramatic possibilities! Then Jesus took the initiative and cried with a loud voice, "Lazarus, come out." This is exactly what can and ought to happen to dead people today (see John 11:38-44).

The place of your spiritual deadness is your daily existence. Your physical body is the tomb of your spiritual death. Jesus, who died for you, rose again, and now lives in the power of an endless life, is prepared to come right where you are and speak with you.

His message is basically simple: "Lazarus" (But perhaps your name is not Lazarus.) "Bill, Marilyn, David, Jean . . ." The word of the Lord must come to you personally. He wants you to admit to being spiritually dead. Then he wants you to be ready to realize your need of him to be life in the place of your deadness.

The next thing the Lord said was, "Come out." Now Lazarus had to do something. As the loud, clear voice of the Lord penetrated his deadness, he had to react against or respond to the authoritative command.

This is exactly what you must do also. If you understand that he has something to say to you and you can understand what he is saying, you must act upon it. Respond to his offer to live, and commit your life to him in order that his life in all the power of his resurrection might be released in you through his Holy Spirit. Alternatively, you can reject his call and command to you, and remain in your deadness.

Lazarus obeyed the command, responded to the call, and "the dead man came out" (John 11:44).

Let's Get Practical

1. What is our spirit created to do?

2. How can we tell whether our church is spiritually alive?

3. How is your appetite for God and his Word? What does that tell you about your spiritual life?

4. Today, how will you show, by your actions and words, that your spirit is alive?

2

The Guaranteed Life Plan

John 3:1-22

If you had the opportunity to talk with the world's greatest theologian, what would you want to discuss? Now imagine you had been alive in the time when Jesus walked the earth and you could have had your conversation directly with him! The things you chose to talk about would reveal a lot about your spiritual understanding (or lack thereof).

The Gospel of John tells us the story of a man who had exactly that opportunity. His name was Nicodemus.

Nicodemus was dead and didn't know it. But he should have known. He had a brilliant intellect; in fact, he was professor of theology at the University of Jerusalem. His training had been of the highest caliber, and he was an outstanding man. It is tragic to know that outstanding men are sometimes dead men, but it is worse to think that they can know so much and yet be so ignorant. Some brilliant men don't even know the truth about themselves! Imagine Nicodemus all those years addressing his students and being dead all that time! He may not have known, but I wonder if his students knew!

All his life, he had meticulously observed all the rules of his religion. And those rules were tough. Carefully he checked the food he ate, the company he kept, the places he went, and the clothes he wore. His religion ruled all these things and many more. He must have been so sincere, so serious, and yet so very dead.

When he spoke in the Sanhedrin, the place of government for his country, he spoke with a great concern for truth and honesty. His integrity was unquestioned, and he was held in high esteem. But the tragedy was that, while he wanted to help govern his country, he couldn't govern himself. This was because he didn't know the most important thing about himself: He was dead!

One dark night he learned the truth. As an honest, intelligent man, he had been most interested in the activities of a young carpenter-preacher who had been making a name for himself. He decided to have a personal talk with the young man.

Of course, a man in his position had to be careful. What would the officials of the university think if they knew he was consorting with an uneducated artisan! It wouldn't be so good if the Sanhedrin found out he had met with a potential rabble-rouser either.

Of course the Pharisees didn't miss too many tricks, and Nicodemus knew he would be the talk of the synagogue if they found out where he had been. So once again, proving that discretion is the better part of valor, he slipped furtively into the presence of the young Galilean, under cover of darkness.

Nicodemus was most gracious. He, the professor, addressed the young carpenter-preacher as "Rabbi." Then he complimented him on his miracles and acknowledged that this man, years his junior, was undoubtedly God's man of the moment.

He was shaken to the depths by the response to his compliments: "No one can see the kingdom of God unless he is born again" (John 3:3). I have often wondered why the Lord was so blunt on this occasion. Was he conscious that Nicodemus wanted to talk theology, while Jesus wanted to deal with the man's soul? I do know that the Lord had no intention of wasting time on trivialities. Here was a key man of learning, position, and integrity, who was as dead as it was possible to be, and something needed to be done—quickly!

Nicodemus knew many things about God. No doubt he had lectured on his names and titles many times. He knew the divine attributes and promises, and he was fully conversant with the theological concept of the kingdom of God. Now the young preacher told the old professor that he might have lectured on it, but he couldn't possibly understand it if he had never been born again. This was shattering news.

Nicodemus thought that he had been in the kingdom since he was eight days old. All his school days, he had been thinking in terms of training in order to serve the kingdom. He had done well in his service from a human point of view. He was a success, and he was firmly sitting in the top of the tree! But if the carpenter was right, he hadn't even seen the kingdom. All these years he had been on the wrong track!

At first glance his response to the "born again" statement seems stupid: "How can a man be born when he is old? Surely he cannot enter a second time into his mother's womb to be born!" (John 3:4) No, Nicodemus wasn't asking a stupid question. I think he was being sarcastic. He was probably thinking something like *Young man, are you trying to be funny? I came here for an intelligent conversation, and you start talking nonsense. Born again indeed! What do you think I am? Do you want me back in embryo form?*

The Kingdom of God

"Unless one is born of water and the Spirit, he cannot enter into the kingdom" (John 3:5). In effect, the Lord was saying, "Nicodemus, I want you to understand that there is something worse than being unable to *see* the kingdom of God, and that is being unable to *enter* it." Of course, some of the confusion in the mind of Nicodemus was caused by the fact that his idea and Christ's conception of the kingdom of God were totally different. While they were both using the same term, they were thinking of different things.

Nicodemus the politician may have been thinking primarily in terms of a political kingdom, with a king sitting on a throne in Jerusalem. Was he thinking of the Romans who had conquered his beloved country and now controlled it? Was he interested in ousting them from the land? David the great king, his successors, and the possibilities of the kingdom's being restored were perhaps what he had in mind.

Little wonder, then, that he was having difficulty understanding why it was necessary to be "born again" to get into *that* kingdom! The theologian in him had some idea of the kingdom of God's being more than just political. He believed that when God's king reigned politically from Jerusalem, then God would be reigning in the world. As far as he was concerned, the king of the Jews was God's agent, and when the earthly king was on the throne in the holy city, then God was reigning through him. Then all the subjects of the earthly king would, through him, be subject to God and, accordingly, a part of the kingdom.

When two men have a conversation and one of them does not understand the terms the other is using, it is more than difficult to get very far. Nicodemus understood neither the term "the kingdom of God" nor what it meant to be "born again." So it wasn't surprising that he was in a quandary about "No one can see the kingdom of God unless he is born again."

Being Born Again

The Lord used the simple analogy of human birth to explain what he meant by the new birth. "Flesh gives birth to flesh, and Spirit gives birth to spirit," he said (John 3:6).

When a baby is born it receives life. But the Lord wasn't talking about physical life any more than he was talking about a political kingdom. He was talking about spiritual life—the life from God deep in the recesses of a person's spirit that makes God real and allows God to be king in the center of that life.

When a baby is born, it is suddenly conscious of a new world. At first it almost appears to regret having arrived. But the new baby can see and hear, and very soon he or she begins to know and understand. That which is born physically is purely physical, but that which is born of the Spirit is spiritual. There is such a thing as spiritual seeing and hearing. A born-again soul can see and understand, often in a remarkable way, deep things of God. They become real to him. Truths that were once dark now become crystal clear. A dull Bible becomes a blazing book.

The Heavenly Family

When a baby arrives, he or she is the latest member of the family. Sometimes we get the impression that the baby is the most important member of the family. But whatever the status of the new arrival, family membership is automatically involved in getting born.

When a person is born again by the Spirit into the family of God, God becomes that person's Father in a wonderfully close relationship. All the joys and privileges of a family belong to those born into God's family. The family has its origins in God. It reaches all classes, through all the ages, in all lands, and will last for all time and eternity. The family of God is fabulous, and God is its Father. His concern is the raising of his children. He cares and protects. His guidance is assured, and he provides all that his children need.

In the same way that, in a healthy family, the children love and respect their father, the children of God reverence and adore the Lord who made them his children. His home is their home. His wealth is theirs. All that he has is available to them as they learn to enjoy it, and all that they are comes under his benevolent control. Their good is his concern, and his delight is their concern. Brothers and sisters abound. Wherever a member of the family goes, in all corners of the world, the family will be represented. Strangers to each other will be knit together when a common bond is discovered through a common relationship to the one Father. Spiritual birth is dramatic, climactic, and thrilling, and it reaches further than any person can imagine.

In essence the message of the Lord was, "Don't be surprised, Nicodemus; I'm not talking about a physical kingdom. I'm dealing with something spiritual. When I say you must be born again, I mean exactly what I say: You *must* be born again. It is absolutely imperative. If you ever want to understand the mysteries of God and experience the reality of God, you must be born again. If you want to enter the kingdom and join the family, you must be born again. There is no other entrance to God's realm and the membership of God's family. The new birth is the only gateway."

How Can This Be?

Scratching his head, his brow plowed with puzzled furrows, Nicodemus asked, "How? How can this be?" This is always the quandary of a dead man: "How can I be born again? How can a man who is physically alive and spiritually dead receive new life? How?

"You are Israel's teacher, and do you not understand these things?" asked the Lord (John 3:10). Evidently, the nation was at a low spiritual ebb if a leading teacher didn't know how to be born again! When the leaders of the church don't know the basics of spiritual experience, it is a sad and dangerous day for the nation. Any nation is blind if it is led by the blind. Dead people don't lead other dead people very effectively. Jesus lived in such a day, and in some ways, so do we.

The Lord then reproached Nicodemus for failing to accept the clear teaching of the prophets and disciples, not to mention his own teaching. "What is the point of my telling you heavenly things, Nicodemus, if you refuse to accept the things you have been taught so far?" (see v. 12). Notice that for some reason, this sincere man had not been prepared to go along with the teachings to which he had been exposed. In all probability the reasons stemmed from pride. They usually do.

The reasons for refusing the truth come in various forms but have the same core. Pride doesn't like to be told it is dead. Pride thinks, *I am good enough for the kingdom; in fact, the kingdom ought to be thankful it is honored by my presence.* So pride doesn't like to be told, "You won't even be in the kingdom." Pride says, "I'm not perfect," but always gets upset when someone says, "That's right, you are not!" There was a certain pride in Nicodemus that was quite understandable, but that doesn't mean it was excusable.

So Nicodemus needed to be told that spiritual experience comes through "water and the Spirit." There has been much discussion about the interpretation of the word *water* in this context. It seems to me that the Lord probably meant something that Nicodemus would have understood. And there is little doubt that Nicodemus, being a religious, educated Jew, would have realized it meant some kind of washing and purifying. To his mind, I think the statement meant, "You must be washed and made clean before you can come into the kingdom—clean from pride and arrogance. You must be purified from the idea that you are good enough even though God says you are not."

Evidently Nicodemus accepted this, for the Lord proceeded. There is no point in proceeding with an explanation of the new birth if people refuse to accept the fact of their sin and the necessity for repentance and cleansing.

Look Up for Life!

The Lord proceeded by means of an illustration very familiar to the professor. Out of the professor's textbook, he took the story of the children of Israel in the wilderness. They had rebelled, rejecting the instructions of God and living in a disgruntled and perplexed state. The serpents came in among them, and hundreds were bitten. The poison flowed in their bodies, and death was inevitable. They were as good as dead, when Moses once again acted on the people's behalf and spoke to the Lord.

Moses was told to make a serpent of brass and lift it high on a pole. Then with a loud, clear voice he told the people that God promised new life to all who would look to the serpent, the symbol of God's promise, and trust God to do what he said he would do. There was nothing new to Nicodemus in this story, but the *application* was new.

"In the same way that Moses lifted up the serpent, Nicodemus, I am going to be lifted up," said the Lord (see v. 14). This was a clear allusion to his impending crucifixion. The Lord was saying that his death on a cross was going to be the means of forgiveness for all those bitten by the disease of sin and suffering—the deadness of spirit that sin brings. His death was to take place in order that sin might be judged and sinners forgiven by God.

Of course Nicodemus knew that some people refused to look at the serpent, and as a result they died. Others said they couldn't understand how a piece of twisted metal on a stick could get poison out of their veins. They died. Some felt that if they couldn't be healed by their own doctors, they certainly weren't going to expose themselves to a quack physician holding a pole up in the air. They died.

Nicodemus also knew that there was a real danger that he might adopt a similar attitude to the remarkable story of this remarkable young man. This young man hadn't died, and yet he wanted him to believe that his death would do something for Nicodemus that religion had failed to do. Nicodemus knew that while he had real reservations, he certainly had no answer to what the young man was offering. Nicodemus decided to be careful that he did not reject the message because he couldn't understand it or because he did not like it. It was important that he did not forget the people in the desert who had done that and perished.

Deep in his heart, Nicodemus knew that the deadness of his spirit was simply the introduction to what the Lord called "perishing." But the Lord said that instead of perishing, he could have eternal life. The offer was stupendous. He was being told in all seriousness and sincerity that if he would only trust himself to the Christ who was to die for him, his sins would be cleansed.

Not only that, but he would pick himself up off the sandy, barren floor of his desert and step out into a new life, the commencement of which could only be described as being born again. The born again part of it was to come through the imparting of the life of God—eternal life. This life would be born in him through the Spirit of God. And it was all for him if he would only take his eyes off himself and look to the one who was going to die for him.

The pressure of those moments must have been intense. Imagine the eminent man, confronted with the fact of his own deadness, haunted by his ineffectiveness, baffled by the news of his error, and now firmly confronted with the necessity of deciding what he was going to do. The quiet, compelling gaze of the Lord and the stillness of the night contrasted dramatically with the turmoil of his own heart and the sting of his conscience.

It is no light thing to be told you are dead. It is no easy matter to decide what you are going to do with the offer of a new start and a new life through a new birth. To receive the life of the risen Christ and to enjoy the forgiveness of sins that he offers is a tremendous step.

Strong men have sweated and brave men have trembled when told that if they want new life they need new birth, and new birth means a new start, in a new kingdom, with a new King. They know who their king is, and they are familiar with his demands. They know the changes that must be made if he is to be dethroned and God is to be enthroned. Nicodemus was on the spot. What should he do? This is the quandary of a dead man.

If you realize, after reading Nicodemus's story, that you, too, are spiritually dead, you face the same choice he had to make. He had been ignorant of how to enter God's kingdom, but after talking to Jesus he lost that excuse. You also are now without the excuse of not knowing. Will you accept Jesus' offer of new life?

Let's Get Practical

1. What does it mean to be "born again"?

2. What is your understanding of the kingdom of God?

3. How are religious authorities today sometimes like those in Jesus' time? What do you think Jesus would confront church leaders about today?

4. If you could have a personal, face-to-face conversation with Jesus, what would you ask him?

5. How can you be sure that you have eternal life?

3

A Costly Bargain

Mark 10:17-22

A young television director showed great interest in spiritual things after pastor and author Stephen Brown's appearance on a talk show. Brown says that after answering some questions for the director,

I looked at my watch and realized I was going to be late for an appointment. I said to this young man, "Look, I have to leave, but let me write down on the back of my card the names of three or four books you ought to read. Read them, and then let's get together for lunch sometime and discuss them." I gave him the card and headed for the door.

He stopped me with these words: "Reverend, I don't believe I will read these books."

"What do you mean, you won't read the books?" I responded. "You were the one asking the questions, and those books might provide some of the answers."

"If I read those books," he said with an unusually high degree of honesty, "I might find that all the things you have been saying to me are true. If they are true, then I'm going to have to change some things in my life, and I don't want to change."[1]

This young director, though spiritually dead, recognized that the Christian life requires commitment of oneself to God, a submission of oneself and all one possesses to God.

Jesus once encountered a similar young man, a member of the ruling Sanhedrin, just like Nicodemus. He came in full daylight, right out in the open, unlike Nicodemus, who crept in by night! More than that, he actually came running! Surely a most undignified method of transport for a member of the Sanhedrin!

When he arrived at the place where the Lord was sitting, to everyone's astonishment, he threw himself at Jesus' feet and knelt before him. This young gentleman was in dead earnest. He didn't care who saw him. It didn't matter to him what people thought of his behavior. His status was forgotten. He was oblivious to the dust on his clothes and the stares of the passersby. There was something on his mind so important that everything else seemed to be irrelevant.

What was on his mind? The first words from his lips give the answer: eternal life! "Good Teacher, what must I do to inherit eternal life?" he asked as he stopped in front of Christ (Mark 10:17).

Three Crucial Questions

This is a most remarkable question, and one of utmost importance. There are many people who do not know what eternal life is, and because they aren't sure what it is, they don't know if they have it. Obviously, if they don't know this, they cannot possibly know if they want it. Others have some ideas about it, but they don't know how to get it. Still more people think it is something they may get when they die—if they have been good enough.

---

1. Stephen Brown, *If God Is in Charge* (Nashville: Nelson, 1983), pp. 57-58.

Our young friend, however, knew quite a few things about eternal life. He knew it existed. He knew he didn't have it. He knew he wanted it. And he knew where to find it. So he knew a lot!

Presumably he had heard the Lord speaking on the subject at some time. From what he had heard, it was clear to him that there was much more to life than he was experiencing. Isn't it sad that this is true of many wonderful people alive at the present time? They are wonderful—but dead.

The Bible says, "I write these things . . . so that you may know that you have eternal life" (1 John 5:13). Notice that it does not say *"hope* that you *might get."* It says *"know"* instead of *"hope";* *"have"* instead of *"might get."* Do you *know* that you have eternal life? If you are not sure, your place is beside the young ruler at the Master's feet, inquiring.

What is eternal life?

Eternal life is not a thing. It is not strictly an "it." Eternal life is a Person. Talking about the Lord Jesus, the Bible says, "He is the true God and eternal life" (1 John 5:20). It is not difficult to see that the term "eternal life" is basically the same as "life of the Eternal One." Not to have eternal life is obviously to be without the Eternal One and his life. And to be without his life is to be dead.

If it is possible for a human being to experience the life of the Eternal One within him in exchange for his spiritual deadness, it is obvious that eternal life is not only important because it lasts an eternity—nothing lasts longer! But it is the *quality* that is especially wonderful. Eternal life is life that lasts for eternity and springs from the person of God himself. *It is the life of God through the Lord Jesus imparted to people while they are still here on earth.* Eternal life has all the quality of God's life.

Do I have eternal life?

This young man had seen the quality of the life Jesus lived, and he knew his life didn't bear comparison. Yet Jesus had very little, while he had everything. Jesus wandered about homeless, but he had a fine home. Jesus had to be on his guard continually because of people who wanted to kill him, while the young man was living in the lap of luxury.

In fact, this strange sense of dissatisfaction was even more remarkable because he had all those things other people desired. His neighbors envied him: *If I had his position I would be happy. . . . Boy, is he rich! . . . If only I had his money, his looks, his personality, and his prestige, I would be the happiest man on earth.* Youth, money, home, and position were all on his side. Security and popularity were his. But his life lacked quality. There was no real sense of belonging. He was empty.

When he came in search of eternal life, he was searching for the "life more abundant" he had heard this teacher had come to give. That was what he didn't have, and that was what he wanted. The eternal life he sought was a life of eternal quality. He wanted to live, and he knew the life he wanted was to be found only in the Eternal One. Do you have that kind of life? Do you have a life that is as eternal in its quality as it is in its quantity? If not, then your place is beside the young man at the feet of Jesus Christ. Your question ought to be his: "Good teacher, what must I do to inherit eternal life?"

How can I receive eternal life?

Jesus started to answer in an indirect sort of way: "Why do you call me good?" Then he said, "No one is good except God alone" (Mark 10:18). Why would he say that? Surely this young man was only being polite?

Evidently the Lord realized that the young man needed to learn that although he was good, he was not good enough. When Jesus talked to Nicodemus, he bluntly introduced the subject of the new birth. On this occasion he did a similar thing. *Not good enough?* But this young man was outstanding. Listen to the conversation (see vv. 19-20).

"You know the commandments, don't you?"

"Yes, Master."

"Don't commit adultery."

"I haven't."

"Don't kill."

"I haven't."

Through the list Jesus went, looking the young man straight in the eye. Under his gaze, a gaze that can strip a man naked to his inner thoughts, the young man never flinched once. "All these I have kept since I was a boy," he said (v. 20).

The Lord was impressed with this fine young man. He felt a tremendous surge of love in his heart for him. But the lesson the Lord had to teach him was that it is possible to be good, but never good enough. The world is full of "good people," but they aren't good enough.

How can this be? It all depends on the standard of measurement. You might be a good swimmer in the pool next door. When people see you cut through the water for about six strokes they say, "What a good swimmer." But how would you make out in the Olympics?

The young man was outstanding by human standards. His friends called him religious. His employees called him fair and kind. His business associates commented on his honesty. But God saw his weakness.

Do you know what his weakness was? The Lord didn't tell him in words. He proved it to him another way. "There's only one thing lacking, young man. I'll tell you what to do if you want to have this life of eternal quality and quantity. Go home and put your home up for sale. When it is sold, give the money away, and then come back to me and we can talk business" (see v. 21).

The ruler's weakness lay in his possessions. "Money is the root of all evil" is one of the most misleading misquotes of the Scriptures. The Bible does not say that. It says, "The love of money is a root of all kinds of evil" (1 Tim. 6:10).

There is nothing sinful about money, and there is nothing sinful in having money. But there lies untold danger in loving it and living for it. People will lie for it, cheat for it, scheme for it, even kill for it. When a person begins to love money and possessions more than anything else, those things become gods. That is where the sin lies.

The young man looked as if the bottom had fallen out of his world. *Sell my possessions and give everything away? But that's unthinkable, unreasonable; I couldn't possibly do that!* he thought.

The Cost of Eternal Life

The Lord had examined him on the commandments, and he had come through with flying colors. However, he had not mentioned the great commandment that stated, "You shall have no other gods before me."

If he had talked about this, the young man would have said, "I've never done that. I have never bowed the knee to Baal. I have never worshipped the gods of gold and silver." But this would have been untrue. He had never been anything but orthodox in his religion, but at the same time his orthodoxy had left plenty of room for other gods. He *had* worshipped the gods of gold and silver. He didn't realize this until he was told to get rid of them. He only learned how precious they were when he was threatened with the possibility of having to do without them. His worship and dependence had never been so real until the ghastly moment when he was confronted with his own slavery to these things. The one God was his God, but only in theory. His money was his god in practice.

No other gods

It is so simple to be good by the low standards of modern society, and it is impossible to be good by God's standards. This does not mean that God is unreasonable. On the contrary, God loved this young man and longed to do something for him. But you can't do something for a person who is not prepared to admit that there is anything wrong with him!

The problem with this earnest, good young man was that he was governed by sin. The greatest sin a person can perpetrate is to deny God the right to be God in his or her life. This was the man's sin, and this is the sin of most people.

Eternal life is available to sinners, but first the sinners must admit that they *are* sinners. Then they must be prepared to turn from their sin. In the case of the rich young ruler, first he had to recognize that he was giving nothing more than lip service to God. Then he had to admit it was sin and be ready, whatever the consequences, to turn from his sinful approach to life. Only when this was done was Jesus prepared to do business with him. With these tremendous truths ringing in his ears, the young man was hardly ready to take any more. But Jesus hadn't finished with him.

Take up your cross

He went on to explain that a person who desires eternal life must also "take up the cross and follow me" (Mark 10:21, KJV).

Many remarkable things have been said about this phrase "taking up the cross." I have heard some people who are afflicted with arthritis saying, "I suppose there is nothing much I can do about it. It must be my cross, so I'll have to grin and bear it." I don't want to appear unsympathetic to any sufferers, but I must say that arthritis is not their cross. It is simply their arthritis.

Often when we talk about bearing the cross, we think that it means putting up with the unavoidable things of life with the bravest smile possible. But this is not cross bearing. When the Lord Jesus took up his cross, he wasn't putting up with something he couldn't escape. He wasn't trying to look as if he were enjoying it when he wasn't. He was abandoning himself to his Father's plan, and that plan included a cross. Jesus took it as a token of his overall acceptance of God's will for his life, even though it was going to be severely painful. Taking up our cross is recognizing that God is God, and Jesus is Lord, and surrendering to the divine plan and to divine ways, regardless of the consequences.

The Cost of a Gift?

Occasionally you hear people talking about the cost of becoming a Christian. Then in the next breath they will tell you that salvation is free! "Eternal life is a gift, but there is a price to pay," they exclaim. How it can be a gift and also require payment, I haven't been able to discover. But we know what they mean. They are pointing out, quite rightly, that accepting the gift of eternal life affects all a person says and does, and that some requirements are hard and therefore are regarded as part of the price that has to be paid.

I think a better way of looking at it would be to realize that the price has been completely paid—by Christ. Having paid the price of our ransom from sin by his death, Christ rose again to offer us life through a relationship with him. Eternal life is based absolutely on him. If there is no relationship, there is no eternal life.

Obviously, if eternal life is based on a relationship to him, then he is perfectly entitled to state the terms of the relationship. His terms are quite straightforward: He expects us to be related to him as he is, not how we want him to be. He is Lord, and therefore eternal life is a relationship that involves acknowledging his lordship. That isn't the cost. It is purely an elementary aspect of the relationship.

. . . and follow me

God is not remotely interested in a snap decision that doesn't develop into an attitude of life. "And follow me," Jesus added. This means that he instructed the young candidate for eternal life to be prepared for a totally new life—prepared to go where God led him. It was going to involve a "going on." New avenues and possibilities were to be explored. Fresh areas of life and adventure were to be opened up as Jesus directed; the man had to be ready for anything.

This was hard for the young man. He rose to his feet. His lined face betrayed the battle raging in his heart. He was torn. He knew what he wanted and how he could get it. He knew how it worked and what he must do. He knew all he needed to know. But knowing wasn't enough. Now he had to *do* what he *knew.* The decision was all his and only his. Not a soul could help him. Not even Jesus could do a thing for him. God was able to do all things, and still is, but he will not break his own rules. And one of his rules is that he allows us the right to choose. Therefore, the young man had the right to choose and the responsibility to choose right. Slowly he turned away, and he spoke not a word. His shoulders hunched; his feet dragged in the dust. He decided in that moment to say no to life. Automatically he said yes to death. He walked away from eternal life. He walked away dead!

If you have not yet made your choice, you need to do so without delay. Like the rich young ruler, you have the responsibility to choose and choose rightly. Your life hangs in the balance.

Let's Get Practical

1. How can we have eternal life?

2. What is it that makes people long for "something more," or for eternal life?

3. How are Christians today like the rich young man? How are we different?

4. What are the things that try to rule your life?

5. If you came running to Jesus today, what do you think he might challenge you to change or give up?

4

Rebels Have Less Fun

Philemon 1-25

Have you ever noticed how kids love to give each other creative nicknames? A child who gets glasses becomes "Four-Eyes." A youngster with a big nose might be tagged "Banana Beak." The child with large ears may be called "Dumbo" after the elephant in the famous children's story.

Sometimes a person's nickname grows out of his own name, which may be unusual or seem inappropriate to the person. The apostle Paul wrote about a person like this in his letter to Philemon.

Onesimus was his name. It's a most unusual name by present-day tastes, and I imagine it was almost unique in his day, too! It means "profitable." Imagine the fun his friends may have had teasing him about his name! Think of the agony he might have suffered as a boy. Every time he did something wrong at school, he braced himself for the inevitable gibes about "profitability" that came his way.

As time went on it became obvious that young "Profitable" wasn't living up to his name. He became a slave in the household of a religious gentleman called Philemon. It was soon apparent that he wasn't going to get along there too well. It could have been the religious atmosphere of the household that got on his nerves. Many people have found that there is nothing quite so irritating as being exposed to religious people in a religious environment when you are thoroughly irreligious yourself. Such was the unhappy lot of young Onesimus.

Naturally, he had many things for which to be grateful. For instance, he had a master who was an outstanding Christian gentleman. His conditions of service were as ideal as it was possible for them to be in those days of slavery. He could have been in far less pleasant circumstances, and even if he didn't appreciate the Christianity, he certainly benefited from the Christian graces of his master.

Longing for Life

Onesimus's main problem was that he had much religion, but no reality. He was the dead man we have been considering. He had all the encouragement and outstanding example that anyone could want, but he lacked life. Poor old "Profitable" was dead. Because the religion that he saw lacked reality for him, he had to do something about it. Being a lively young man, he did the predictable thing—he rebelled.

Often I have seen young people exposed to and sometimes hammered by religion that was meaningless to them. Nine times out of ten they have rebelled. In fact, I believe that if a young person has any spirit in him at all, he will most likely rebel against religion that appears to him to be suited to the elderly middle classes rather than the up-and-coming young people who have their lives to live.

Living his life was uppermost in Onesimus's mind, as one would expect. He didn't relish the thought of surrendering to the God of whom he had heard so much. He found that there were many more attractive ways of living open to him. Religion on the outside, and latent rebellion on the inside, meant a most uncomfortable turmoil for the young slave. I expect he made many other people uncomfortable at the same time!

It only needed a spark to cause the explosion. Onesimus decided that enough was enough, and he packed his bags and left Philemon,

Colosse, and religion, to get out into the big world and live. The craving of the dead is always for life. So he ran to look for it.

Running from God

Onesimus wasn't just running away from people and situations. He was running away from God. That, of course, is a common phenomenon of the human race, and a ridiculous one as well. It is possible to run from God, but it is impossible to get away from him, as Onesimus was to discover later. But still the rebellious run. They cannot see that their only hope is in running *to* God: "Come unto me . . . and I will give you . . . ," he says. But in their minds they say, *Let's get as far as possible from him, because he will rob us of all that we think is important and spoil all that we want to do.*

Robbing God

The mention of robbing, of course, leads us to the next part of Onesimus's decline. He was short of funds for his journey. Religion had taught him to respect other people's property, but the pressure was on, and his desire to run was too great. The visions of "life" he had conjured up burned brightly. He lost control, and he robbed his master. This was also quite predictable. When a man is desperate, nothing is sacred. A man's principles are always subject to revision and rejection when there is the possibility of those principles' thwarting his desire. He knew better, but he robbed. In his position as a slave, this was about the worst thing he could do. He was doomed. So he ran all the harder.

In a strange sort of way, people also rob God. In fact, anyone who rebels and runs automatically robs God. This may sound ludicrous, but it is perfectly true. Some would even say, "How can a person rob God?" This is exactly what they were saying in Malachi's day. God explained then, and his explanation still stands.

We rob God when we keep to ourselves what is really God's property. God reminded them about tithing. In those days people were expected to recognize that one tenth of their earnings (before tax!) was not theirs at all. It was God's. People then were like us now—they were greedy. So they began to withhold the tenth, thinking that they were simply choosing not to give something that belonged to them. But they weren't. They were holding back from God what was his. That is blatant robbery!

God also accused the people of robbing him in another way. They were giving to him things that were inferior, such as lame sheep. With a pious smile on their faces, but with a keen eye to business, they offered animals for sacrifice that were of no market value. God called this robbery. This kind of robbery is not uncommon today. Where is the man or woman who can say, "I have always given God his due and have never kept back anything that belongs to him"? Where are the men and women who can honestly say, "I have never relegated God to an inferior place in my life, and I have never given him anything but the best"?

Rome or Bust

"Rome, here I come" was Onesimus's magnificent obsession. And to Rome he went. He had a great time there, and no doubt he thoroughly enjoyed himself. Sometimes you hear preachers saying that people like Onesimus aren't having a good time. These preachers either haven't tried it, or it is so long since they did that they have forgotten what a great time some people do have in their sin. What they probably mean is that the great time doesn't really satisfy. Neither does it achieve anything except a transient enjoyment that disappears all too quickly.

Onesimus was having fun, but in the depths of his conscience there was a nagging fear of the consequences of his sin. His enjoyment was constantly flavored with unpleasant thoughts that his inner man wouldn't let him forget. The dead man is happy—when he is happy. It is those times when he doesn't have the necessary entertainments or distractions that cause him most trouble. Then his conscience troubles him, and he has no peace. The conscience of our young friend was spoiling his vacation in Rome, and there wasn't anything he could do about it. Then came a remarkable coincidence that wasn't a coincidence.

Busted in Rome

There is no doubt in my mind that this "coincidence" was a piece of magnificent engineering. It was the work of a Genius who was busy bringing two men together, even though neither knew that the other was in the vicinity. This is part of God's specialty. He knows the hearts of people, better than we know ourselves. He was fully conversant with the inner workings of young Onesimus, and Onesimus was an open book to God. The runaway slave's mad search for life had not escaped the all-seeing eye of the young man's Creator. Nor had the heart hunger that was driving him remorselessly into one foolish escapade after another.

God cared in a practical way. So he looked around for someone whom he could trust to get in touch with the desperate youth. His choice was Paul. This was apparently a strange choice. If you were sending someone after a runaway thief, would you send a theologian? If you needed to cut short the drunken vacation of a reprobate young man, would you send a missionary? Perhaps you wouldn't, but God did.

It all depends on what you want to do with the youth when you have found him. If you want to bring him to justice, you send a policeman and throw him in jail. In Onesimus's case, this would perhaps have meant execution. If you want to teach him a lesson and get him off the drink or drugs and away from his unsavory friends, you send someone tough, who can handle a rough situation.

But God doesn't work our way, because he is interested in achieving more than justice and rehabilitation. He is concerned about the remaking of ruined lives, not just salvaging them. That being the case, he has to send more than an officer of the law or a social worker. A spiritual man is needed, who can not only deal with the legal and social problems of the case, but handle the deep, spiritual root cause of the problems. Paul was the man for the job.

God is expert at organizing the circumstances of people in such a way that he can do something for them. I remember speaking once in a coffee bar full of young people who would not go near a church. The bar was crowded with all types of teenagers. I was speaking about Onesimus, and when I had stopped talking, a girl of about sixteen years of age came to me and said, "I'm rebelling against everything. I robbed my mother this evening. I took all her money out of her purse. Now I'm on the run." Her story perfectly fit the story I was telling. She drifted into the coffee bar not knowing anything about it, and I spoke about the young man whose experience fit hers, without knowing anything about her. Coincidence? I don't believe so, because God sends people to get in touch with the spiritually desperate.

Now, I don't think we have any reason to assume that God said, "Paul, go to Rome, and on the Appian Way you'll find the young slave that you met at the home of Philemon in Colosse. Get him and take him back to Philemon. He's on the run." No, I feel certain that Paul was in Rome as part of God's plan for his life, and that, as always, he had his eyes wide open for opportunities to be an instrument of God's blessing wherever he went. He was so well acquainted with the "strange coincidences" that regularly happened in his life that he now recognized them as part of the divine plan. In fact, he anticipated this sort of thing. He wasn't surprised anymore. Paul had long since learned that anything can, and probably will, happen when God is in control.

When Paul saw young Onesimus so far from home and obviously "living it up," he thought, *Hello, and what exactly is that young man doing here?* He found out the easy way, by going up to him and asking him! The youth on the run must have had the biggest shock of his young life. The thing he had dreaded more than anything else since he went on the run had happened: He had been caught. Immediately he began to wonder how much Paul knew. Had Philemon sent him? Was it any good trying to bluff his way out?

"What are you doing here, Onesimus?" asked the preacher.

"Vacation," might have been the unconvincing answer.

I don't know how long it took to get the real story, but eventually it came out. "Paul, I got tired of everything. I wanted to live. I felt as if I was in a straitjacket. I rebelled, I ran, and I robbed."

The Way Home

Of one thing I am certain. Paul did not say, "Tut, tut," and launch into a three-point sermon! This young man had no need of a sermon. He was caught, and he knew it. He was fully aware of his sin. The awful truth of what he was and what he had done filled his mind. "What can I do, Paul?" he asked. That is the question that Paul was waiting for! It is the question that the Lord loves to hear, for it is the question of a dead man who is at the point of realization.

Repentance

All was not as well as he thought. He was in need, and he didn't know from where his help would come. Simply and searchingly, Paul reminded Onesimus of the things he had already heard. "You will have to repent, Onesimus. In case you aren't sure what it means, it means make an about turn in the way you are going, and let God be God."

Onesimus replied, "I'll do that."

Restitution

But there was something else that had to be done. Repentance in his case involved restitution. He had to return to the place of his crime and put right what he had done wrong. He had to repay what he had stolen. Restitution is the stuff of which repentance is made. If you meet someone who claims to have repented but who is not prepared to put right what he has done wrong, then it is doubtful you have met a real penitent.

"I'm ready for that, Paul," Onesimus said. "Yes, I'll go to Philemon and I'll take what's coming to me. But Paul, I don't know where I'll find the strength." This was the heart cry of the crest-fallen youth.

Receiving Christ

He didn't have the strength yet because he hadn't received the Lord Jesus, who would infuse life into his deadness through the Holy Spirit. He was a stranger to the strength the Lord gives to all who receive him. Paul showed him how to thank Christ for dying for him personally. Then he led him in a simple prayer asking the risen Lord to come into his life. Immediately Onesimus was born again, and his crazy search for life was ended. Believe it or not, he had found life in the very One from whom he had been running! And when he received Christ, he received the strength that he needed in order to be different.

Responsibility

Is this the end of the story? Not at all. It is just the beginning! The man who was now Onesimus's spiritual father took his new responsibility seriously. He fed him and helped him, encouraged him and advised him. He gave him plenty to do, and Onesimus rose to the occasion. Eventually, when Paul felt the time was ripe for Onesimus to take a deep breath and go home, he found that he didn't want to part with him. Onesimus had become Paul's right-hand man.

Paul's sense of humor comes out in the letter of explanation that he sent with Onesimus to Philemon. He said, "Do you remember young 'Profitable,' who was a dead loss? He has now become as profitable as his name. He is a tremendous asset to the kingdom. Receive him, and forgive him for my sake. There has been a revolution in the man" (see Philem. 8-16).

Revolution

Of course, it is only to be expected that there will be a revolution when the risen Lord gets into a person's heart through the new birth. New interests and appetites will be seen. New power and energy will be released. The new birth will change a dead man into a living man, a complete person who has a contribution to make.

Let's Get Practical

1. Where does religion without reality lead?

2. Why do people try to run from God?

3. What are some ways we can rob God?

4. If you ever "ran away," like Onesimus did, from the responsibilities and realities of your life, did you find the life you were seeking? What did you learn from your experience?

5. The path that Onesimus took started with religion without reality that led to rebellion. This made him run and rob. Then came the moment of realization. Repentance and restitution followed. He received Christ and was revolutionized. Where are you right now on that path? Where would you like to be?

5

The Easy Way to Misery

Luke 15:11-32

Let me tell you the story of a modern prodigal. This young man grew up going to church, and he had a godly mother who loved him, told him about Christ, and prayed for him every day. But he rejected his mother's God, and he left the rural community in which he was raised to seek his fortune in a large city far away.

His whole focus was materialistic. He was working to build a fortune for himself, and he had no interest in a God whose existence he didn't acknowledge. The faith and prayers of his mother seemed wasted as he pursued only money and possessions.

Then some friends brought him to a dynamic, vital church, and there he came to see the emptiness and futility of the life he had been leading and the goals he had been pursuing. As he realized his need, he came back to the Jesus his mother knew and loved, and he became a child of the heavenly Father.

A couple of years after this man returned to the Father from whom he had earlier walked away, God gave him a vision for a tremendous work that would reach literally millions of people for Christ and that continues to do so today. The name of this former prodigal is Bill Bright, founder and president of Campus Crusade for Christ.

The world's most famous prodigal son story was told by Jesus and recorded in Luke 15. This young man's basic problem was selfishness. His father had great plans for him, but he wasn't interested in them. The only thing that concerned him was getting what he wanted in life and totally disregarding all other considerations. This is the essence of selfishness. And selfishness always brings a person, whether a Christian or non-Christian, into defeat.

Many Christians are continually conscious of a battle going on within them. One part of them wants to do one thing, and another seems to be pulling in the other direction. Part of them has a desire to be what God tells them to be, and the other part won't allow it. Something inside them hates some of the things that they do and wants to stop doing them. Something else inside makes them do the things they hate. They find in themselves a continual battlefield. It almost seems as if they have a dual personality.

In a way, this is exactly what a Christian is. He has two natures, or powers, within him. One is the tremendous power of self, which obviously can only be selfish. The other is the power of the life of the indwelling Lord Jesus through the Holy Spirit. These two powers are in continual conflict. When the power of self is in command, the Christian will reproduce an un-Christlike, selfish life. On the other hand, when the life of the living Lord is being demonstrated, it is the result of the power of God's Holy Spirit being in control.

The Path of Selfishness

The young man in our story was a sad picture of a defeated, selfish Christian, whose experience we will do well to note. It is always good to be able to learn from other people's mistakes. In fact, that is one reason the Bible is so careful to record the failures of the Lord's people—in order that we might learn from them.

Asking

The story begins with a young man going to his loving father and asking him to give him what he had already promised. Now, there is nothing sinful about that. At first sight it would not appear that he was being particularly selfish. Surely a boy is entitled to go to his father if he needs something, and if his father is a good father, he will be delighted to do all he can. True, but this youngster actually had the audacity to suggest to his father that he would like to have his share of what his father was going to leave in his will, and he wanted it immediately. He couldn't wait for his father to die! He needed the money! Did you ever wonder what the father thought? We will never know, but we do know what he did. He granted his son's request.

If there had been any doubt about the caliber of the son when he asked for his inheritance, the doubt disappeared the moment he got his hands on the money. Totally regardless of the effect of this action on his father, he packed his belongings and left home, taking his money with him. This was selfishness par excellence.

You can see how clear a picture this is of the behavior of a Christian whose life is controlled, not by the gracious Spirit of God, but by the merciless dynamic of self. "Heavenly Father, give me this and give me that" is his common prayer. But what is done with what God gives is of tremendous importance. Blessings are not given to Christians by a benevolent God solely that the Christian might be blessed. He intends that the one who has been blessed should use the blessings he has received to be a blessing to others. The Christian who is always getting and never giving is living in the suffocating grip of self-absorption.

Attitude

Attitude is also very revealing. If a person appreciates what he receives, he invariably shows his gratitude in some definite way. If he doesn't, it is certain that he has not been very appreciative. To be the recipient of God's goodness without a corresponding warming and softening to the Lord's wishes and desires is definite evidence of a selfish heart. "God I need you and your blessing, but I don't want your plan. So please would you save my soul, forgive my sin, and take me to heaven when I die? But Lord, please don't ask me to be what you already told me you want me to be. I do have my own plans, you know." That is the language of a Christian as despicable as the young son in the story.

It was this attitude on the part of the son that not only made him impervious to his father, but also landed him in a far country. He got himself as far away from the influence and presence of his father as he possibly could. I suppose if he had seen the grief on his father's face, even his cold heart might have thawed a little. But he couldn't afford to thaw. His plans were made. If he had seen the development of his father's business and the responsibilities that were his, he might have experienced some pang of remorse or some slight prick of conscience. But his conscience needed to be chloroformed, and distance was the safest anesthetic. So to the far country he went—out of sight, out of contact, out of reach of all that home and family represented.

When a born-again child struggles with the overpowering self-ishness of his own heart and loses the struggle, the Holy Spirit doesn't leave him. A son can be as bad a reprobate as possible, but he will still be a son. The father might even take the step of disinheriting a disgraceful son, but the son will still have the life of the father within him. Likewise, the Holy Spirit isn't idle in the heart of the selfish Christian. He is continually speaking, revealing, reminding, and suggesting. The selfish saint will do all he can to quiet him, but to no avail. The conflict of conscience and the awareness of sin from his convictions will reach even into the farthest country.

Activity

The greatest desire of the type of Christian about whom we have been talking is to silence the voice of the Spirit. To do this, he has to make certain that his mind is busily occupied. He will try to drown the holy voice with other voices that are tuned to the loudest possible volume. He will live as hard and as fast as he is able. He will multiply his interests and activities, and if he really works hard enough, he might even be successful. But what a waste!

The activities and interests this person uses as anesthetics will invariably be of secondary importance. (If he is a Christian, everything is of secondary importance to Christ.) So he wastes his potential. He doesn't realize it. He misses the point of his life, and he fails to be what he was created and redeemed to be.

The tragedy is that he will know this deep within. In his quiet moments he will be painfully aware of all he is missing, and his conscience will trouble him. So off he will go again in an ever increasing flurry of escapades and activities. He is caught in a relentless spiral that drags with increasing power into a life of utter waste and disgrace.

Awareness

One day the young son went to his secret hoard for more money and discovered the bags were empty. He had no more money to take. He was broke. It must have been a horrible feeling. He was now far from home, without any real friends, living among strangers who didn't care, out of contact with his father, and not a cent to his name. No doubt his mind flashed back to the day he was made rich by his father. He thought again of the sight of his wealth laid in neat piles before him as he counted and recounted it. The way he'd parted company with his father's hard-earned savings troubled him. The sheer waste and tragedy of his folly swept over him. He was sick at heart.

Then something even worse happened. The utopia to which he had fled suddenly ceased to be utopian. The golden city fell on hard times. In the place of well-dressed, well-fed, happy-go-lucky crowds filling the streets, emaciated, pitiful beggars began to appear. They weren't looking for a good time. A good crust would satisfy them. The dreaded famine had arrived. Hunger in its awful intensity gripped the city, and desperation filled the hearts of the people. The young man was in a worse state than most. He began to be in need. He needed help financially, medically, physically, socially, and above all spiritually. But there was no one to help. The irony of his situation was that he had all the help and love that he could possibly wish for back home, but he didn't want that kind of help. In his heart there was still a stubborn insistence on going his own way, independent of his father, and in this way he continued, although the only certainty for him was tragedy.

His heart was no different from the heart of any Christian who has a job or work to do and is not prepared to do it. They all go through the same agony of spiritual bankruptcy. They all know the gripping pains of insistent spiritual hunger. Failure and tragedy are no strangers to them, but still they persist in a policy of estrangement from their heavenly Father. In pigheaded fashion, they drag themselves on to increasing chaos and waste, and all the while their Father waits to give them overwhelming blessing and possibilities of real fulfillment for them in his service.

Surely most people who see the truth of this in their own lives get back from the far country as quickly as possible and make a new start. The son in the story didn't. He actually went farther away. Desperate in his need, he cared not where or how he found help—except, of course, from his father. That was out of the question. So he threw himself on the cold charity of a citizen of the far country. It was obvious that his new employer wasn't remotely interested in him. He was only concerned about getting a man to do the job that no one else was eager to do—feeding pigs. It also looks as if the young man was expected to live with his charges and eat with them. Isn't it amazing how low people can sink?

Spiritual Bankruptcy

When you know the perversity of the human heart, including your own, this may not seem so amazing. Children of God are tragically adept at sinking into spiritual bankruptcy. In fact, whenever a child of God gets into an attitude of rebellion toward the Father and lives in rank selfishness, he or she is in a vulnerable state. He or she, driven by lack of spiritual reality and hounded by selfish desires, will search hungrily for someone or something to relate to.

The realm of relationships with the opposite sex is a common realm of spiritual sinking. So many Christians have sunk to such unbelievable depths because they allowed their desires and hungers to run riot. They have been governed solely by selfish and sensual considerations. The control of the Spirit of God in these matters was neither sought nor found. For many it has meant the end of a ministry. Others have known the heartache of a life that never fulfilled its God-given function. When Christians join themselves to citizens of the far country and neglect the Father who made them, they ask for trouble and invariably get it.

I have met many of the Lord's people who are perplexed because the Lord has allowed certain things to come into their lives— a divided home, a broken marriage, business failure, and many other things. I believe these things have happened more often than not because the Christians acted in selfish disregard of the Lord's wishes and commands and have reaped what they have sown. It doesn't do any good to ask why God allowed your marriage to be a continual battle if you insisted on marrying someone who wasn't the Lord's. There is no point in blaming God for business failure if your business practice was diametrically opposed to all the Father desired for the conduct of your business.

Evidently the pigs weren't as hungry as the son, for he was able to get hold of some of their food and steal it from them. Imagine the heir to a fortune stealing a pig's dinner! Perhaps the pigs let him take it because they felt sorry for him! If they did, they were certainly kinder than the people around him, for none of them gave him anything.

Seeing Ourselves More Clearly

There was a turning point in the sad saga of this young man. He had a vision. It wasn't a particularly startling vision. In fact, all that happened was that he got an excellent view of himself as he really

47

was. He could have had that vision at any time during his mad career, but he didn't, possibly because he was too blinded by other considerations.

It is difficult to get a glimpse of one's own spiritual condition when one is wrapped up with all kinds of other things. In fact, a person usually has to come down to the rock bottom of self before he can really see himself.

His vision wasn't a pretty one. But neither is any realistic vision of self in all its horridness. Scene after scene flashed through his mind—his childhood, his big ideas, his conflict between what was right and what was wrong, his despicable behavior to his father, his wasted opportunity, his sin. All this together gave this young man his first real glimpse of himself.

What to Do about It

Having seen himself, he then had to come to terms with himself. It is one thing to see the truth about yourself, but another thing entirely to be prepared to admit it and do something about it.

Have you noticed the striking similarity between the story of Onesimus and this story? On reflection it isn't really surprising. The same power that drove Onesimus, who wasn't a born-again person, was at work in the young son and is still at work in the lives of born-again Christians. The self and sin that ruined Onesimus can still run riot in us. Of course we have the counteracting dynamic of the living Lord within us, but if we live as if he were not within us, we will be guilty of the same sin and selfishness as the non-Christian. This is the reason for much so-called Christian behavior that is sometimes of a lower standard than the behavior of those who don't know the Lord.

A well-disciplined though unregenerate person can be more winsome and helpful, kind and considerate than a Christian who has ceased to operate under the influence of God's life in him or her. Many people are perplexed by this strange fact, but they needn't be. God doesn't eradicate the power of sin when a person is born again. He gives us the Life that is greater than our sin, but if we refuse to live under the power of the Life, we will be a disgrace and a stumbling block.

We Christians desperately need to "come to ourselves." There is a great, great need for an awakening of Christian vision—vision of what we really are, vision of what we ought to be, and vision of what God will do in and through us if we let him.

Let's Get Practical

1. What does it often take for people to realize their tremendous need for the heavenly Father?

2. What do you think has caused some of the "spiritual bankruptcy" you have observed?

3. Why do believers still tend to be driven by sin and selfishness?

4. How can we see ourselves more as God sees us?

5. As you reflect on the story of the Prodigal Son, what observations can you make on your own life? What are some steps you need to take to draw closer to the heavenly Father today?

6

Why Coast When You Can Charge?

John 5:1-15

Joni Eareckson was a beautiful teenage woman full of the energy, enthusiasm, and bright dreams that youth have in such abundance. She pictured an exciting life for herself in the years to come, and she had every reason to think those dreams would come true. In one instant, however, all that was changed. A diving accident left her a quadriplegic for life, virtually paralyzed from the neck down.

When Joni was injured, she faced a tremendously challenging decision. She could withdraw emotionally, curse God, wallow in self-pity, and let her family take care of her for the rest of her life. Or she could praise God, determine to make her life count, and set out to discover how he wanted to use her in spite of—or maybe *through*—her disability. The challenge was before her, and the choice was hers alone. It was a hard challenge but a clear one, a choice between vibrant life and inward death.

Jesus presented a similar challenge to many people during his earthly ministry, and one such story is related in John 5. One day he met a man who had spent *thirty-eight years* lying on his back. It was at the place called Bethesda. Many of the unfortunates of

Jerusalem used to gather in that place daily. It must have been a depressing place. Crippled people, emaciated and forlorn, huddled in pitiful groups. Beggars were there, trying to eke out a miserable pittance. The bitter and the hopeless rubbed shoulders with the weak and dying. There was a continuous hubbub of moans from the suffering, mingled with the shrill cries of the beggars rising higher and higher in an effort to be heard above their fellow sufferers.

The House of Mercy

Bethesda means "The House of Mercy," and for this reason the pool of Bethesda is a picture of the place where Christians are to be found—the church. A Christian is a person who knows the difference between justice and mercy. There are many people who feel that their lives are up to standard, and they trust that God will do the right thing by them and treat them fairly in the day of judgment. These people hope for the justice of God. The Bible, however, teaches that the justice of God spells out certain condemnation and eternal separation from God's presence for the lost. This is perfectly just, for God not only gave his law, but he outlined the penalties for failing to keep that law. Justice demands that the right penalty should be passed for the right crime. Anyone who wants justice from God will get it, but it won't be the kind of justice they hope for. Justice means that God metes out to people what they deserve.

Mercy is exactly the opposite. Mercy means that God recognizes our guilt, forgives it for Christ's sake, and then gives us what we don't deserve—new life and rich blessing, the certainty of heaven and the presence of his Holy Spirit. The mercy of God deals with a person in a way he or she doesn't deserve. Only sinners who repent and claim the effectiveness of Christ's atoning death come into the place called the House of Mercy.

There is a further interesting point about Bethesda. You arrived there by means of the sheep gate. This reminds us of the Lord Jesus, who said, "I am the door of the sheep." He insisted on calling people sheep. Sheep are about the most stupid animals on God's earth. They follow each other without thinking. They push their way through hedges built to protect them. They don't seem capable of recognizing when they have things provided for them, and they always wander, seemingly aimlessly following the one in front. When you think about it, the Lord knew what he was talking about when he called us sheep!

Of course, when a sheep comes under the control and care of a shepherd, it becomes a totally different animal. It seems to be content and placid. The desire to wander disappears, and the sheep appears to appreciate all the shepherd provides.

Jesus explained that he is not only the Shepherd who organizes the sheep, but he is also the door of the sheep. In others words, he claimed to be not only the source, but also the entrance to all the blessing to be had in the House of Mercy.

The pool

Just inside the House of Mercy was a placid pool. It was calm and still, soothing and peaceful. It was the sort of pool that you could sit by for hours and let your fears and anxieties sink into its depths. That is exactly what many Christians enjoy about being in the place called Bethesda. They attend the services and enjoy its ministry, and the calmness and stillness of the setting quiets them and fits them for further excursions into the busy world. Perhaps this is why some churches choose the name Bethesda. Personally, I don't think I would ever be happy choosing that name. I'll tell you why.

The porches

Bethesda was divided into five compartments, and in these compartments lay many people who did very little else but lie there. Sometimes I feel that this application of the story is a little too true for comfort! The church does tend to be divided on many issues. Obviously, there is much to be said for both sides of most arguments, but we in the church spend too much time arguing about our different departments instead of uniting as much as possible against a common foe. I can imagine some of the people who have been lying in the porch for thirty years, refusing to move to another area of the pool simply because they belong where they are, and no one is going to move them.

A few years ago I visited a town in England that possessed five churches, all belonging to the same denomination. Someone suggested that as the average congregation in each church was approximately ten, it would be good to unite. There would have been room for the united congregations to sit comfortably in the choir loft of any one of the churches, but the idea was rejected. Why? Because these people had all been sitting in their porches for so long that they preferred to stay where they were.

The posture

The posture of the congregation at Bethesda was significant, too. I once had a friend with a remarkable philosophy. He used to say, "Never run if you can walk. Never walk if you can stand. Never stand if you can sit, and never sit if you can lie down." When he was lying down he was happy. Presumably he was happy because lying down is the last word in inactivity. This congregation before us was regular in attendance but tragically inactive. They lay there and did nothing. I am sure that many recognize this as an amazingly accurate picture of many pew-occupiers. They have entered the place of mercy but have assumed an attitude of indolence and idleness that is shocking to behold. Why is it that so many of the Lord's people are perfectly happy never to lift a little finger in the Lord's service? Where do they get the idea that they are doing fine as long as they join the congregation around the pool and do nothing?

The problems

The description that follows rings a bell. The saints at Bethesda were blind. We usually reserve the idea of blindness for the unconverted, but Paul showed in his letter to the Ephesians that it is not uncommon for converted people to be blind. They need their eyes opened to depths of truth of which they are ignorant. Maybe you recognize there are vast areas of spiritual understanding that remain dark to you because you are blind. You may admit that you are lame like Lazarus and many of the congregation at Bethesda. And when you realize that the standard of spiritual development the Bible talks about is so far from your own condition, you also realize that the description of "paralyzed" fits as well. Blind, lame, and paralyzed!

What can the recumbent saint do? He or she can wait for something to come from somewhere in some way! There is a wonderful spiritual exercise called "waiting"—"They that wait upon the Lord shall renew their strength" (Isa. 40:31, KJV)—but that kind of waiting doesn't mean hopeless inactivity. It means dependence that anticipates blessing. The Bible talks about "waiting for God's Son from heaven." That means an eager looking forward to his return, coupled with a desire to be busy when he comes. That definition hardly fits the congregation at Bethesda.

The worst word used to describe the people in the House of Mercy is "invalid." In the Greek it means literally "no dynamic." The sort of dynamic that makes things move is the sheer power of God. This sort of thing is happening in isolated parts of the world, but it is not the common experience. The church of God, composed of born-again children of God, is intended to be a living organism that demonstrates nothing less than the overflow of divine power that shows itself in mighty floods of blessing. It isn't happening in many areas because Bethesda is populated with "invalid" folk.

It is easy to be critical, and I have no desire to be offensive or destructive. But I assure you that I am saying this because I believe it, and also because I believe that something can and should be done about it. Impotence and idleness must be exposed. Defeat and death must be recognized.

When Jesus Comes

The Lord moved into Bethesda one day. It is significant that he didn't work on a congregationwide basis. The contrast between the words "a great multitude" and "a certain man" is startling.

If anything is to be done about the Bethesda situation today, it will have to be done on the individual level. Congregations are made up entirely of individuals, and the only way in which a congregation can ever be affected is when the individuals are altered. We should always remember this.

Next time you feel that the "church" in general is at fault, check to see that the fault is not in you. Churches and congregations are only as strong as the individual members that compose them. Therefore, the only way to deal with the problems of the whole is to deal with the integral parts of the whole—and that means you and me.

Could it be true that your church is what it is because you are what you are? Is it possible that the effectiveness or lack of it in your church is measurable in terms of *you* multiplied by the total attendance? The Lord wants to deal with the undynamic individuals who are responsible for an undynamic church.

The account of the Lord's visit says that he saw what was going on. He also knew all about it, and he said something in unmistakable fashion. This is searching truth. You find the same thought in the book of Revelation, where the Lord dictated some personal letters to various churches. He explained that he had been watching, that he had evaluated the situation, and that he had something to say. Never forget that he knows better than anyone how inactive and lacking in God's life you may be. Not only that, but he is adept at evaluating the causes and the consequences of this lack of liveliness. He is ready to talk to us about it. His words will be straight to the point as always, and there is no doubt that they will search hearts. However, we need to be ready to expose ourselves to the sharp, cutting edge of truth in these days of need. If anything is going to be done to get men and women off their backs and onto their feet, it will be done when recumbent Christians are prepared to listen to what God has to say.

Are You Willing?

I'm sure that this man had been asked many questions during his thirty-eight years by the pool, but the question the Lord asked him was a revelation in itself. "Do you want to be made whole?" he asked.

Think about it for a moment. He could have said many different things, but he chose to ask a man who ostensibly could think of nothing else but getting himself cured, "Do you really want to be made fit?"

It is possible to lose the desire or will to get well after a long illness. Helplessness often leads to hopelessness, and this may be what the Lord had in mind. Why would a man who spent all his days at the place where he might be made well have gotten himself into a situation where he might not really want to be made well? Possibly because inactivity can become very attractive. Some people discover that the less they do, the less they want to do. Maybe he thought, *Now if I say that I would like to be healed, he might heal me. Then I wouldn't be able to lie here any more. I would have to become energetic and busy, and I don't know if I would like that.*

Or there is the problem of responsibility. As an invalid, the man had everything done for him. Friends carried him and cared for him. They provided for him, and he enjoyed their goodness. He had no cause to worry, for they did the organizing and the worrying. A man in that condition is in danger of becoming a parasite. His thoughts might have been, *If I get better, I will no longer be able to let them do everything for me. I might have responsibilities of my own. I don't know if I want to be burdened with responsibility. I must be careful that I don't get healed and then regret it because of all that I will be expected to do.*

This is the message to invalid saints: "Do you really want to be made powerful and dynamic through the power of God in your life? Or would you much prefer to be able to stay in an unusable condition so there won't be any risk of having to give up something for the sake of God's plans? Do you feel that God might put you into a situation that might mean your private life has to be altered, so it would be safer to stay an invalid and then there won't be the same risk? Has your evangelical niche become so comfortable or so calm and still and the porch so reassuring and safe that you would not be willing to have the Lord ruffle your water and disturb your stagnant calm? Christian, are you really willing to be made whole?"

"It isn't all my fault," you may answer. "If you knew my church and the unfriendly atmosphere, you wouldn't talk like that. You don't know how much we've tried different approaches, and they weren't successful. I don't think you can expect much more than what we are doing. When you've said it all, you must remember that we are living in days of apostasy. We can't expect too much in these terrible and difficult days."

This sort of answer no more answers the question than the invalid man's answer. He made the same sort of excuses, blaming everyone but himself. He suggested that he had done his best and that it wasn't his fault that he was still lame and powerless. If the people had been quicker and more helpful, he might have had a different story to tell.

Up and At 'em!

Jesus altered his approach. He ignored the excuses and the moans. He didn't ask any more questions. He spoke with great authority and issued a command: "Stand up, pick up your bed, and start walking." There comes a point in the Lord's dealing with his people when he starts to issue commands.

The Lord's people have great ability in discussing problems and forming subcommittees to present reports to other committees, which will then refer them to another committee for clarification. Then resolutions will be passed and conferences arranged to discuss the implications of the clarifications of the subcommittee's report to the main committee. It might be better sometimes if we gave a golden handshake to a few committees and did what the Lord told us to do!

We must have organizations, and we need committees and committee people. But when talking becomes a substitute for obeying, it is time to realize that to fail to do what the Lord says is disobedience, and disobedience is sin—even if it is dressed up in the orderly cloak of organization. The Lord may cut through our delaying tactics and give a command, and then the pressure is squarely on us.

The command he gave seems ludicrous. If the man could walk, he would not have lain there for thirty-eight years. What was the point of telling the man to do something that everyone knew he couldn't do? Had the Lord taken leave of his senses? No, there is a great lesson here for us all.

The Lord never gives a command that we ourselves can fulfill. But he also never commands us to do anything that he himself cannot perform. He makes available to us all the power of his ability when he commands, so that it is possible for us to access his power at the moment of his command. Then we can obey and do what for us is otherwise impossible. This is good news for defeated people, dormant at Bethesda.

With this command ringing in his ears, the man had to decide what he was going to do. Obviously he knew that the Lord was capable, and he sensed that he was willing. Therefore, the onus was on him to act upon what he knew. The challenge rested squarely on his emaciated shoulders. He decided that he wanted to be different. He chose to allow the Lord to work in his life, knowing full well that all sorts of repercussions would follow. Making use of the strength of the Lord himself, he did what he was told. He stood up. He grabbed his bedroll. He stepped out—straight into trouble. But the person who does what the Lord says and allows the Lord to take away his invalid status always expects something to happen, and he is never disappointed.

Jesus gave complete physical healing to the man at Bethesda, but he did no such miracle in Joni Eareckson's body. Instead, she accepted his challenge, and he did a far greater healing. He cleansed her spirit of the pride, bitterness, anger, and self-pity that could have destroyed her. And in their place he gave love, joy, hope, and faith. He also gave her an ability to communicate powerfully those same qualities to millions of people in a most remarkable ministry.

Will you accept the Lord's challenge? Will you let him heal your spirit and give you new life, *even if you have some physical problem he doesn't heal?*

Let's Get Practical

1. What is significant about the meaning of the word *Bethesda?*

2. What kind of people would gather there?

3. How is the church like the pool at Bethesda?

4. How are you like the people at the pool?

5. If Christ were to come to you today and "make you well," what do you think his next words to you would be? What would he tell you to do?

7

Your Arms Are Too Short
to Box with God

Genesis 32:22-32

Are there times in your life when you are made especially aware of
your sinfulness? Perhaps you struggle with a bad habit that continually reminds you of your weakness. Maybe you know some
saintly person and you see your failings in the light of his or her
purity. Or have you had one dramatic experience that brought you
up short and made you face your rebelliousness and the disapproval
of God?

The Need to Be Made Right with God

Our God works in various ways to make us aware of our sins so
that we will seek reconciliation with him. The Bible tells us of a
number of these confrontations between sinful people and a gracious Lord who wanted to bring them into fellowship with himself.
Paul's encounter with the resurrected Jesus on the Damascus road
is perhaps the best known of these. But an Old Testament story,
found in Genesis 32, tells of a man who had made a practice of lies
and deceit all his life before God challenged him face to face.

Jacob had been made painfully aware of his own sinfulness on more than one occasion. His history was one of unfailing defeat. Over the years he had staggered from one crisis to another and had perpetrated every trick in the book. No one, not even his own father and brother, had been exempt from his sharp practice. He made enemies easier than friends, and he knew that awful experience of having no one to turn to in his hour of need. He was one of the most needy men of his day.

The Need to Be Made Right with a Brother

After a long time evading the consequences of his malpractice, he decided that the time had come for him to face the music. So he reluctantly gathered together his family and possessions and started the long trek home. Wily as ever, he sent scouts on ahead to see what sort of welcome he could expect. Their message didn't help at all. They told him that Esau his brother, looking grim, was marching in their direction with four hundred henchmen, looking equally grim.

Strategy was called for, and as usual Jacob had a plan. He organized a massive present for his brother. More than five hundred and fifty prize animals from his herds were gathered together and driven in the direction of his formidable brother. The herdsman in charge had his instructions to see that Esau had no doubt about the sender of the present.

Of course, Jacob knew that he had cheated his brother out of more than a few hundred animals, and therefore he wouldn't have been surprised if the gift (or bribe) was rejected. So he took further precautions. He divided his considerable wealth into two separate bands and sent them by separate routes, figuring if he lost one he could always make do with what was left. He also worked the same principle with his wives, women servants, and sons.

Then, having taken all the precautions he could to protect his own skin and his own wealth, he settled down for the night. That is, he tried to settle down. One would have thought he would have no sleep that night for worrying about his wives' wandering defenseless into the path of his furious brother. It is reasonable to assume that the thought of his eleven young sons out in the cold, dark night would have kept him awake. But there is no evidence that this was the case. Jacob was as safe as he could be—but he didn't sleep. He had a visitor.

An Encounter with God

Before we think about the visitor, let us spend a moment looking at Jacob as he sat alone in the dark. His thoughts troubled him. As he looked into the future, he was understandably afraid. There didn't seem to be much hope for him. He had no one to blame but himself, but that didn't make him any less afraid.

Then he had time to reflect. As he looked back over his life, he thought of the tremendous advantages he had enjoyed. The blessings that God had sent his way came before him. Like a drowning man, he saw his past life flashing before his eyes. And he was ashamed. He knew that he had squandered his advantages and abused his blessing.

People have a habit of becoming reflective when they are left alone in the stillness. They tend to become almost melancholy when they sit down and think. That is why they don't like to be left alone with their thoughts. They switch on a radio the moment they enter a room or drive off in their car. The television is indispensable when they have an idle moment. If neither is available and friendly company is not at hand, they stick their head in a book. But they hate to be left alone with their thoughts, because their thoughts often trouble them.

Jacob was in this frame of mind when his unexpected visitor arrived. The Lord himself visited Jacob in that lonely place. Be careful to note the position. He was afraid of the future, ashamed of the past, and alone. Then the Lord arrived. We are not told how the interview started, but we do know that it developed into a wrestling match. It takes two to make a fight, so while the Bible says that the Lord wrestled with Jacob all night, it is obvious that he wrestled because Jacob resisted.

Wrestling with God

This is a most remarkable thing. Imagine Jacob in that sort of a situation, wrestling with God. He was not wrestling with God to try to squeeze some blessing out of him, but wrestling because he was resisting God with all his strength. He had absolutely nothing to lose by surrendering to God, and he had everything to gain. What could be worse than his situation at that moment? His past was a disgrace. His prospects were gloomy to say the least. His heart was gripped by an awful sense of loss and shame. He had a golden opportunity to put things right with his God, who had taken the trouble to visit him personally.

There was no one around to hinder. He could never wish for more ideal circumstances to have dealings with the Lord. The Lord was anxious to help and to bless. And all Jacob could do was fight. He fought God as hard as he could. The battle went on all night. While we must see the folly of Jacob's action, we must also admit that it takes quite a person to wrestle with God through a cold, dark night.

The person who resists God knows—as no one else knows—the coldness and darkness of his spiritual night. Nothing seems to make sense. Nothing satisfies. Everything appears hopeless, and the more he struggles the worse everything becomes. But still he wrestles.

It is quite a few years since I did any wrestling, but I can still remember the basics. There are many different styles, of course, but the main idea is to get the opponent on the floor and keep him there. I suppose that is the position of defeat—flat on the canvas, unable to move. The difficulty comes in that your opponent not only wishes to make sure that you are unsuccessful in your attempt, but he also insists on trying to put you on your back! So you have the strange situation of two people trying to do the same thing to each other while they are both trying to stop the other from doing it. Complicated? Yes, but great fun if it is only sport.

There was no entertainment value in what Jacob was doing. He was trying to stop God from having supremacy over him, and he was trying to gain the advantage over God. This was stark lunacy, but he fought on.

The apparent stalemate is only resolved when one is able to outwit the other or to overcome him with superior strength. Obviously God could have slapped Jacob down at any moment he wished, but he was gracious enough to give Jacob the chance to submit of his own free will. This is always God's way of dealing with us. He could obliterate us at any given moment, but if he did, he would defeat his own ends. He wants the glad submission of his subjects, not the unwilling capitulation of rebellious serfs.

Resisting God

Wrestlers have to move and think quickly. They need to be able to recognize an attack, resist it, and turn it to their advantage all in one fleeting moment. They get a hold on the opponent's head. He obviously doesn't like it and resists by putting a merciless hold on the other wrestler's arm. No one likes anything by this time, so one trips the other. But at the moment of the trip, as they are both in midair, one twists the other underneath and wins the fight.

In his dealings with Jacob, God switched his point of attack continually. He got a grip on Jacob's sin and said, "Jacob, submit." He got hard, unrelenting resistance. So he left his hold and switched to Jacob's past. "Admit your failure," he said, but resistance was the only response. And so on he wrestled, graciously, persistently straining to bring his rebellious child to the point where he could do something with him—the point of submission.

As the dawn began to break at the close of that dark night, God came to the reluctant conclusion that he was getting nowhere with Jacob. This is one of the most fearful things I have read concerning God's dealings with us. To think that God can be thwarted so long and so violently that he decides there is nothing to be done about the person he is longing to win! I believe it is possible for a child of God to be so persistent in rebellion that God decides not to struggle anymore. In a sense it is as if God says, "All right, you have shown me quite clearly that you will not accept my plan and acknowledge my lordship. You obviously want to go your own way, so I will let you have your will." This may sound like people gaining victory over God, but it isn't. It is God graciously allowing us the right to exercise our own will and have our own way. God isn't the loser, but we certainly are.

Getting hurt

When the divine Wrestler came to this conclusion, he touched the hollow of Jacob's thigh and dislocated it. I am sure that Jacob immediately lost all interest in wrestling! The dislocation of the smallest member of the body can cause excruciating pain, but the agony of a dislocated thigh must have been unbearable. The proud wrestler couldn't lie down quick enough. He was beaten, and he knew it.

Of course, God could have started in this way. He could have moved straight into battle and put Jacob down in one easy movement. But he chose not to do it that way. The Lord is always much happier when his child submits voluntarily rather than under compulsion. Obviously the willing surrender brings more joy to the heart of the child of God, too.

Whenever Jacob looked back to the night of his fight, he would always be reminded that he gave in to God because he had to, and not because he wanted to. This would color his attitude for the rest of his days.

God still has to act this way. If a Christian insists upon being useless to God, then God in all probability will feel it necessary to place the rebellious one in such a position that he will not get in God's way. He may have to put him off to one side, where he will cause the least possible trouble. This does not mean, however, that he loses his salvation. Service is the point of consideration here, not salvation. His salvation is secure, but his service will be null and void.

You can see what God has in mind in the letters he wrote to the churches in the book of Revelation. He said that it might be necessary to remove the candlestick, meaning that he would terminate the effectiveness of the church's ministry and witness. Incidentally, if you look for those churches today, you will have difficulty finding them. It would appear that the Lord was forced to do what he said he might have to do.

Relenting

Then the silence of the night was broken by some ghastly words, "Let me go." It wasn't the rebellious Jacob who said that. It was the Lord who spoke. He has gone as far as he could with Jacob, and he was prepared to move into other lives that might prove more willing and amenable to his desires. "Jacob, let me go; I am moving on. You have been struggling all these years. Now you can have what you wish—complete freedom to go your own way."

The words bit deep. Jacob was suddenly confronted with the possibility of being given what he wanted. The right to determine his own destiny, for which he had fought so long, was his. And he didn't want it. Do you think he was being capricious? Was he always changing his mind and never knowing what he wanted? No, that wasn't his trouble. He realized in a flash how much he needed the Lord and how hollow everything would be without him.

Receiving God's blessing

His answer revealed his true thoughts. "I will not let you go unless you bless me." Jacob had a great need of blessing in his life, and he knew it. Also, he was fully aware that the only one who could make real the blessing he needed was the one who was about to leave him to his own willful stupidity. Now he was desperate. There was nothing he wanted more than the fullness of God's blessing on his life. The transition couldn't have been greater, and it couldn't have come quicker. In a twinkling of an eye, his heart was changed.

There is no deliverance from defeat and no fullness of blessing for the rebellious and the halfhearted. Those who hunger and thirst after righteousness are the ones who are filled. It is the thirsty who come to Christ and drink of him who see the rivers of living water flowing from their lives. There is nothing superlative about the Christianity of the wavering, halfhearted, divided saint. There is only defeat, heartbreak, barrenness, and regret.

But Jacob was different now. He longed for all that God had for him. The reason he changed his mind was that he realized he was useless. He was crippled and alone. He was vulnerable and defeated. He was friendless and aimless. He was consumed now with the emptiness of his spiritual condition, and it all came about through a dislocated thigh.

No doubt you know of instances in the lives of Christians similar to this. Perhaps they have been confronted with some tremendous challenge, stricken with some overwhelming sorrow, or crippled by some disease. It may be that they have gone gaily along their barren pathway for years, and it was only when they were put on their back and shown in no uncertain terms the uselessness of their lives that they faced up to reality. If you know people like this, and you also know that as a result they became desperate for the blessing of God in overflowing measure in their lives, you are fully aware that they wouldn't have missed the experience for all that the world could offer them. They will testify to the fact that the blessing resulting from their sorrow, disappointment, or disability made everything worthwhile.

Have you come to the point of surrender either through the pressure of circumstances or through a heart that is hungry for God? Have you laid hold of God with all the intensity of your being and said, "God, I'm desperate for you and your best, and I will settle for nothing less." This is the pathway out of defeat.

Confessing

But the Lord hadn't finished with Jacob. "What's your name?" he asked. Strange words indeed! Surely the Lord knew. Anyway, it was hardly the time for introductions.

Quietly came the answer, "Jacob." The answer was more than just an acknowledgment of his name. It was an acknowledgment of his character. It was a confession. "'Twister,' that's my name. 'Contriver and Cheat,' 'Warped and Corrupt.'" Jacob was actually telling the Lord, with deep contrition, what he really was. And that was music to the ears of God.

Did you know that one of the things the Lord loves to hear is the full and frank confession of our lips? Are you aware that the Lord longs for you to come to the point of admitting what you are? Has he heard it from your lips?

Changing

Listen to the thrilling response of the Lord: "You are no longer 'Twister'; you are now Israel, 'Prince of God.'" Then the Lord gave his reasons for the change of name. "You have power with God, and you will have power with men. You couldn't possibly be called 'Twister' when you are going to be the sort of man who can be the means of the power of God being released among people. You have prevailed, Israel. Through admitting defeat you have gained the victory, and you are going to be triumphant. Twister isn't the name for that kind of man."

What exciting words, and what thrilling prospects for Israel! But this is the sort of exciting thing that God loves to do. He specializes in this kind of transformation. This is exactly the kind of miracle he plans for you. Let me remind you when it came about and how it came about. It all started when Jacob surrendered unconditionally to the Lord. Then his heart attitude changed. *Instead of defiance to God, it became reliance upon God.* His resistance became dependence. God can and will make any Twister into a prince when the Twister is hungry to be different—hungry enough to agree to the total control of his God upon his life. Then the twisted one must realize that utter dependence upon his Lord assures full supply of all his needs. This attitude allows the Lord to move into business.

Of course, that isn't the end of the story. It really begins there. Israel named the place to remind him of the fact that he had met God face to face. It became holy ground to him. But that wasn't his only reminder. He had the other reminder with him for the rest of his days—he limped on the leg that had been dislocated. From that day on he never took a step without the evidence of his surrender that led to victory. I can imagine his saying, as he went down on one leg, "That reminds me of the day I was put on my back." Then, as he inevitably rose on his other leg, he thought, *Praise the Lord, for he raised me up and made me walk in a new way.*

What memories do you have of wrestling with God? Perhaps you have physical scars from alcoholism, drug addiction, or some other sinful activity. Maybe there are emotional or psychological hurts that have never healed. Or it could be that you're still fighting against his lordship in your life even after years of his patient efforts to win your devotion.

Will you learn from Jacob's example? Will you surrender control of your life to the loving heavenly Father who has your best interests at heart? Will you give up your rebelliousness against a God who deserves instead your loving obedience?

Let's Get Practical

1. Why do you think Jacob wanted to make things right with his brother?

2. What do you think is the connection between reconciliation with God and reconciliation with other people?

3. What does it take for reconciliation to occur between people or groups who have somehow hurt or alienated one another? How can we work toward reconciliation in the body of Christ today?

4. If you have ever "wrestled with God," what did it take to bring you to the point of surrender? How did this change your life?

5. What do you need to do today to make things right between you and God or to bring healing to a relationship that has been broken or hurt in some way?

8

The Secret of Supercharged Christians

John 8:31-36

Joe is typical of many Christians today. You might recognize some of his story in your own life. There is no doubt but that Joe is born again, that he possesses spiritual life and is part of God's kingdom. But he is a believer whose life gives little evidence of spiritual power.

The problem is that Joe is controlled by bad habits like laziness and procrastination, and by sinful attitudes like self-centeredness and materialism. Joe knows these things are wrong, and that makes him feel guilty. He also knows they rob his life of effectiveness in matters of lasting value, and that makes him miserable.

But no matter how many times and how many ways Joe has tried to gain victory over those habits and attitudes, he always fails. He just can't change himself. He has almost given up hope that his life will ever be different.

As we have seen, this can be the experience of those who have been born again. They aren't dead, but they aren't winning in the battle against the sin nature; they are defeated. Does the Lord have anything to offer to defeated saints like Joe? Or is defeat the normal experience of those who come to newness of life in Christ?

The answer comes loud and clear in the great shout of the Lord outside Lazarus's tomb, "Loose him and let him go" (John 11:44, KJV). The Lord does not intend for those who are born again to spend the rest of their days on earth bound and gagged, defeated and disillusioned. He has laid plans for his redeemed people that will enable them to live in the liberty he gives. His idea for his born-again children is for them to thoroughly enjoy their salvation and to thoroughly revel in the life he gives on earth while they are making their journey toward heaven and its eternal glory. I believe the great cry of the risen Lord today is "Take off the grave clothes and let them go!"

Tied Up and Frustrated

No one had to tell Lazarus that he was frustrated. His bondage was obvious to him and to everybody else. This is a rather sobering thought. The church needs to recognize that when a person is bound and beaten, it is perfectly obvious to the onlookers. People, for all their cynicism, are watching Christians. They profess to be disinterested, but under cover of these protestations, they keep a keen eye on what Christians are doing.

One day I asked a young Englishman, "Do you ever go to church?"

He looked at me in amazement and said, "You must be joking!"

"No," I replied, "I am perfectly serious."

His reply was shattering. "Look mate," he said, "I'm miserable enough. I don't want their misery. I have enough problems of my own without any more."

Then he told me how he had stood outside a church on Sunday mornings watching the people go in, and waiting for them to come out. He added, "You want to know something? They looked as miserable when they came out as when they went in."

Now, I am well aware that it is easy to be critical, but I think this young man had a point. He watched, and he evaluated on the basis of what he saw. He saw nothing that impressed him. Perhaps he saw what the people outside Lazarus's tomb saw. Both he and they recognized defeated people when they saw them.

Kinds of Grave Clothes

There is nothing that binds the life of a Christian that the Lord Jesus cannot overpower. There are no such things as grave clothes that he cannot tear away. Once the Lord has been given the opportunity to do all he can do with the Christian who is having trouble, there is no limit to what he will do. But first he must have a willing, submissive person who is ready for anything.

Those we want to keep

Some grave clothes cling tightly. There are relationships that bind and blight and yet are tremendously attractive to the one who is bound. There is no liberty for the person who finds the grave clothes more attractive than life in God. No released life will ever be enjoyed by a person content with bondage and unconcerned with the life that Christ intends to live in them. Desire and aspiration play a tremendous part in the life of the person whom the Lord will set free.

Those we want to lose

Some grave clothes appear to be so strong that people who long to be rid of them fear it is an impossible hope. They are convinced of the mighty power of the Lord to do great things in a general sort of way, but they have absolutely no expectation that he will do anything with their problem.

Take the grave clothes of temperament, for example. Some people bound by and to a bad temper are terribly conscious of what they are and what they do. Often they get sick at heart after an outburst they could not control. But instead of letting the Lord do something, they try to excuse themselves with such inanities as,

"Well, I suppose it's my nature, and I'll just have to learn to live with it. You must remember, of course, that my grandfather had a bad temper, and my aunt Agatha had red hair, so what hope is there for me?" There is *every* hope for them, if they will come to terms with the words of the Lord.

Free Indeed!

How does it work? This is the question we are all bound to ask in these circumstances. The answer is found in the words of Paul to the Roman Christians. "Through Christ Jesus the law of the Spirit of life set me free from the law of sin and death" (Rom. 8:2).

This may require a little explanation. The "law of the Spirit of life" refers to the principle whereby the Holy Spirit makes the life of the risen Christ real in the lives of all those who receive him. When Nicodemus was born again, he was born of the Spirit. In other words, the new life he received came through the entrance and invasion of his spirit by the Holy Spirit. At the moment of his conversion, he received the mighty Holy Spirit, who would work in his life to overcome the power of sin.

The old power of sin and self uncontrolled can only lead a Christian into defeat, but when the Holy Spirit is allowed to have his way in a believer's life, the sheer dynamic of his life can and does overcome. In this way there is deliverance from bondage. Only in this way is it possible for the Lord to say, "Take off the grave clothes and let him go."

Do you have a burning desire to be released from the sin that binds you and the habits and failings that trouble you? Do you believe the Lord can handle the problem? Then you must speak to the one who lives within you by his Spirit and ask him to set you free. But you need to ask in a special way. It is possible to ask God to do things and never to expect anything to happen. It is useless asking God in this way. You need to ask him to do what he has promised to do, stating the promise, and then thanking him that he will.

I well remember a young man who was a member of a group that my wife and I took to Holland for a conference. He had a problem with smoking. Every evening he used to go alone to a quiet canal for his evening cigarette. The boy was absolutely addicted and had been since he was about twelve years old. In fact, he smoked so heavily that he had to manufacture his own supplies.

One night I talked to the group about the words of the Lord Jesus when he stated, "You will know the truth, and the truth will set you free" (John 8:32). Then I showed that when the Lord said the truth would do the emancipating, he was referring to himself, for he added, "So if the Son sets you free, you will be free indeed" (John 8:36). Obviously he was using the term *truth* as a description of himself. I tried to show the young people that whatever was binding them in their Christian experience, the Lord through his indwelling life could and would set them free.

Unknown to me, there was a hungry boy listening. He was hungry to be rid of the habit that was his master. He heard that a Christian is a person who has a power greater than any other power within him. Therefore, he knew that for him to claim to be a Christian but at the same time to be dominated by a lesser power than the Spirit of God was a contradiction. So he evaluated his grave clothes and knew that they had to go.

As usual, he went down to the canal. But for the first time he went there longing to be set free. He did an unusual thing. He took out his cigarettes and threw them into the canal, one at a time. As each cigarette fell into the water, he repeated the words that he believed with all his heart: "So if the Son sets you free, you will be free indeed." He testifies to this day that the Lord had the victory over this thing.

Naturally he still had many battles over this problem. Many times he longed for a calming, soothing smoke. The Lord hadn't taken away his desire, and the Lord hadn't given him a new strength of will power. Every time he claimed the promise of God, however, and each time he counted on the adequacy of his Lord, he was set free.

I am not suggesting, of course, that smoking is a heinous sin. But in all fairness I would say that I don't like the habit, and that when a Christian is in bondage to it he is living a contradiction. I am simply using this as an illustration of the possibilities and also the means of liberty that can be experienced in the place of bondage. Perhaps you have never smoked in your life, but something else dominates your life. What is it? The Lord wants to set you free. Is that what you want?

Let Go

I am so glad that the Lord Jesus added, "and let him go." These words hold a tremendously exciting thought for me. Have you ever fired an arrow from a bow? What do you do? The first thing you do is to load the bow with the arrow. Then the string must be drawn back until the tip of the arrow reaches the front of the bow. Then you simply loose it. What do you do next? Drop the bow and run after the arrow, pushing it? Do you try to keep up with it so that you can encourage it? No, of course not! You loose it, and you let it go.

You see, the moment you loose the arrow, the power that is linked to it automatically takes over. It does it with such enthusiasm that the arrow defies other forces and speeds with tremendous velocity toward its target. The moment of release is the moment of new momentum. Listen again to what the Lord said: "Loose him and let him go" (KJV). This is exactly what happened.

Lazarus had a fantastic power within him. It was the power of a resurrection life given to him by the Lord Jesus. This life had not been allowed to express itself until the moment of release. But once released, that was it! All the new life had been waiting for was a chance to get moving. And when the chance came, the chance was taken. Lazarus really began to go!

You are in a similar position. The moment you claim release from your bondage through the work of the Spirit within you, the dynamic of this same Spirit is ready to propel you in a new path of triumph and victory. Christians don't need more power to "go" in their Christian lives. They need to have grave clothes removed and to depend on the power within them. They need nothing less than the power of the resurrection life of the Lord himself.

Isn't it a tragedy that there are so many Christians who have never realized they have within them all the thrilling power of the risen Lord? Obviously, there is only one person who would want to hide this from the Christian's eyes—the devil himself. He knows that once Christians find out about this, they will really get moving. When the indwelling life within them is released, he will be in for real trouble. So he blinds people's eyes. He persuades Christians that grave clothes are normal. He tells them they are doing quite well, even though everyone else knows they are falling around gagged like Lazarus. This is one of the masterpieces of deceit. Has he deceived you?

The Remedy

In the case of Lazarus, things began to happen immediately. The released man stepped out with a smile on his face and a glint in his eye. He had tasted death, and he knew what life was. He had seen the reality of the afterlife, and he could see the bewilderment of those still on earth. Now he was familiar with the facts of the things confronting every person, and he knew the remedy. He could not rest until he had shared what he had discovered.

I have met so many men of God who spent all their time trying to instill some sense of burden into the people in their charge. They use all kinds of methods to try to stimulate enthusiasm, but they admit failure. Mission secretaries tell stories of needs that are not being met. Veteran missionaries speak of no one to replace them when they retire. What happened to the concern and the burden that used to be talked about?

I am not sure what happened, but I know how it can be remedied. Show a man, woman, boy, or girl the possibilities of the risen Lord's "cutting loose" in their lives. Enable them to come to terms with him. Then move smartly out of their way! For when a person is loosed, that person will go! You won't have to manufacture burden or produce concern. When the Lord is moving in a person, there will be no lack of either burden or concern. Nor will there be a shortage of power.

The World's Response

So great was the impact of Lazarus that the crowds began to congregate. They wanted to see the reality of this new life with their own eyes. Anxious people gathered around him to hear him speak of his experiences. Crowds of seeking people came to him to be shown how they could experience the reality of the Lord in their lives. Many people came into the kingdom. The Lord was in business in no uncertain terms.

There is something thrilling and exciting about a person who is caught up in the full flow of the life of the Spirit. Things happen and continue to happen. Many predictable things result, and the most unpredictable, too. People begin to be drawn to the one who so obviously demonstrates the blessing of God. Hungry souls congregate, and the angels rejoice. There is joy in heaven and blessing on earth when men and women are loosed and let go.

But don't think it is all honey. When the Lord gets busy, his enemy does, too. Satan has nothing to fear from defeated Christians. In fact, he is rather fond of them. They cause him no concern, and they give people plenty of arguments against their Christianity. He doesn't lose any sleep when defeated saints play right into his hands. But if they once get moving, so does he! And that spells trouble for them.

The stir caused by Lazarus was so great that the chief priests got their heads together, and believe it or not, they plotted to put Lazarus to death. Poor old Lazarus had only just got himself resurrected, and they wanted to put him back in his tomb! This must be one of the dirtiest plots of all time!

Why did they take him so seriously? Because he was turning people from darkness to light, and from the power of Satan to God. He had to be exterminated because he was dangerous. He wasn't dead anymore. And he wasn't defeated. He was dangerous!

Three Kinds of People

Paul talked about three classes of people recognized by God. He called them natural, carnal, and spiritual people. Here we have the same picture. Natural people are spiritually dead. The carnal are defeated. And spiritual people are dangerous. I believe there are only three kinds of people in God's economy—the dead, the defeated, and the dangerous.

You may feel you aren't defeated, but you know you aren't causing the devil any loss of sleep. Sorry, if you aren't dangerous, you are defeated.

You might say, "We can't all be dangerous in the forefront of the battle." I can't think why. You live among people, don't you? They need a glimpse of reality, don't they? The risen Lord lives in you by his Spirit, doesn't he? The promises of God apply to you, don't they? Then don't make excuses. If you aren't dangerous with all these opportunities, you are defeated.

But remember the words of the Lord that make the defeated dangerous—"Loose him and let him go!"

Let's Get Practical

1. What is God's plan and desire for his people here on earth?

2. How does he make it possible for us to live this way?

3. What are some things that keep God's people tied up and frustrated in their Christian life?

4. What are some specific ways that the truth sets us free?

5. What habits or attitudes keep you from being "dangerous" in your Christian life? How will you start, today, to let God's Holy Spirit set you free from these things?

9

You Can Make a Difference

Acts 6–7

Charles Colson is a dangerous man—dangerous to the cause of Satan. He is going into prisons around the world, bastions of satanic power, and leading men to a saving faith in Christ by the hundreds. He is also, through his speaking and writing, calling everyday Christians to a deeper level of love for and commitment to the Lord. God is working through Colson's energy and wisdom to make a tremendous impact in our world.

Colson stands in a long line of men and women who have advanced the cause of Christ down through the ages. One man in particular led a life about which I never tire of reading. His name was Stephen, and he was a leader in the first church in Jerusalem.

I find Stephen's story, recorded in Acts 6–7, to be one of the most exhilarating I have read anywhere. No tale of fiction can match this story for action and color. I have yet to find a story that has greater suspense and that records more manly courage than this one. But I think the main reason I like it so much is the challenge it brings to my own heart.

Let us spend a few moments learning from Stephen—the man who was so dangerous that the devil had him put away as soon as he got into his stride. It is important to note that Stephen was not an apostle. His ministry was not specifically preaching and praying. Stephen was appointed by the early church to be a Christian businessman.

There was a certain amount of welfare work to be done in the early church. People began to complain that they were being overlooked and were not getting their share, while others seemed to be getting preferential treatment. Evidently the apostles had more work than they could handle, so they decided to appoint some men who could look after the business affairs of the church while the apostles concentrated on the spiritual matters. Stephen was the first man appointed under this scheme.

There are important issues involved in this turn of events. We, the church, are not making a very great success of evangelizing the world. On many fronts we are retreating instead of advancing. In numerous countries, including my own, the church has lost her grip on the people and has become so remote that most people disregard her unless they want a white wedding, a socialite christening, or a decent burial.

While there are wonderful saints of God scattered far and wide in distant and often dangerous lands, we cannot help knowing that on the whole the supply of missionary candidates is drying up. The support for these fine people is not always forthcoming, and they are constantly hampered through shortage of funds and equipment. The picture is not too encouraging.

In the land where the gospel appears to be spreading more rapidly than any other, Brazil, the situation is not all rosy, either. For even in Brazil there are more people being born every day than are being born again. You don't need a degree in mathematics to see that the gospel is losing ground there. Now, if we are losing ground even where we are most effective, what does it mean? It means we desperately need a mighty movement of God in our people, reaching out to the uttermost parts of the earth.

But where are the people? They are sitting in churches on Sunday and behind desks on Monday. Some of them attend Sunday school on the first of the week and live on campus every other day of the week. Others work in the women's class on the Lord's day and labor in their home every other day. In short, there is no real shortage of people to do the job, for the people who know the Lord are to be found in all walks of life, in every stratum of society, in thousands of geographical locations.

The men and women in business are the people who need a vision of how dangerous they can and ought to be in their secular lives. It is my firm conviction that we must work in these days for nothing less than the total mobilization of the total congregation. At the moment we have the ludicrous situation of one or two people doing a work that is humanly impossible, while hundreds of others are busy making money. It is the people in the pew who hold the answer to the problem of getting the message to the people. Our major need is not more people in the pulpit, but more dangerous men and women, moving out from their pews.

Let us pause for a moment at this point. How many people regularly attend your place of worship? How many areas do they represent? How many people do they touch in their working week? How many others do they contact in their social life? How many homes are within the vicinity of homes represented in your congregation? If you take time to count all these contacts, you will get a surprise. There is a ready-made mission field already within easy reach of your church. Mobilized properly, your church congregation could see mighty victories for God and resounding defeat for Satan.

We must assume, of course, that the businesspeople, the students, and the school children know what it is to be loosed and let go. Seldom do I ever face a congregation of the Lord's people so neat and spruce on a Sunday morning without thinking of the untold and unknown potential wrapped up in them. Very rarely do I fail to be thrilled at the possibilities latent in a well-dressed, well-mannered, well-educated congregation when I think of where they will be Monday morning. I am sold on the conviction that there is yet time to get the message with which we have been entrusted to the people who need it most. But it will only be done through dangerous people. We need Stephens.

Irreproachable Character

There are three aspects of Stephen's life that are of value to us. First, his character was irreproachable. There is no substitute for a life of consistency and conviction. Dangerous Christians are those who live out their faith in the eyes of others in such a way that people know, by watching them, exactly what they believe and what difference it makes to their behavior.

The world is full of Christian-watchers. Stephen was known by the people of Jerusalem. There was nothing underhanded about him. He was a Christian—he knew it and they knew it. He was unafraid and unashamed. He saw no cause to be defensive, so he went on the offensive. There was nothing apologetic about him, so he took a dogmatic stand. Please note that when I use the words *offensive* and *dogmatic,* I do so in the richest sense of the words. His was a virile, dynamic faith that was a constant challenge to all who knew him.

This was the opinion of the Christians in Jerusalem. They were called together by their leaders and told to find an honest man, reliable and suitable for their purposes—a man whom everyone could trust. And immediately they chose Stephen. The people in the pews knew him for what he was.

His character was vouched for, not only by his Christian brothers, but also by his enemies. They hated him with a bitter hatred, but they respected him. Nowhere does the Bible give Christians grounds for expecting all people to love them, but we ought to expect our lives to instill respect in the hearts of God's opponents.

In the midst of his bookkeeping, Stephen found time for preaching and witnessing that was setting Jerusalem alight. Even the temple priests were getting converted by the score. Quite understandably, the dignitaries of the synagogue got more than a little concerned. Stephen was hauled before the council and grilled by those bitter, angry men. They argued and threatened, cajoled and blustered, all to no avail. Stephen was adamant and unshakable. They tried to catch him with words, trip him with arguments. Still he held his ground. In desperation they bribed rogues to bring false evidence. They watched his reaction carefully, and they saw his face become like that of an angel.

I'm not sure what an angel's face looks like, but I have an idea that there was a serenity about Stephen at that moment of tremendous pressure that made many a hard heart miss a beat. Even his enemies saw the reality of his life and were impressed. This is the caliber of a dangerous man. The devil gets shaky when he sees a man like this let loose and let go, for he knows the havoc this type of person can cause wherever he goes.

A Miraculous Life

It wasn't only Stephen's character that made an impression, however. His actions were also irrefutable. Who he *was* constituted a challenge, but what he *did* also caused the devil problems. The sorts of things this pen-pushing deacon did are described for us in Scripture as "great wonders and miracles."

Stephen was a man of energy, a man of action. He had the ability to make the sparks fly. I have no idea what sort of wonderful things he did. If God had wanted us to know, he would have told us. If he had said that Stephen raised a few dead people and healed half a dozen paralytics, that would have made us feel good. We would have said, "Good old Stephen. He lived in the age of miracles. Pity I don't, but there it is. I live in the day of small things. I can't expect anything much to happen these days."

It doesn't say anything about that kind of miracle, so there is no excuse for us. Wonderful and miraculous things still happen today when dangerous men and women are let loose. Don't you think it is wonderful when broken families are reunited, when drunken men are made into responsible men? Isn't it thrilling when dope addicts are set free and give their lives to the service of others? Isn't it a miracle when an adulterous wife is converted and her life is put in order? I am certain that Stephen saw this kind of miracle in his day whether he saw the more spectacular kind or not. These miracles happen today and ought to be happening through your life.

The beauty of a life that is responsible for wonders and miracles is that it cannot be dismissed. People can argue theology until the cows come home. They can discuss the psychological implications of mass evangelism *ad infinitum*. But there is little argument to be made about changed lives and salvaged homes, rescued families and new people. That is the value of a life that works wonders. It not only brings blessing, but it also silences the critics. Or if it doesn't silence them, it makes their words sound foolish and empty. Dangerous people perform actions that are irrefutable.

Irresistible Words

There is one other thing about this dangerous man that I would like to mention. His words were important; in fact, they were irresistible.

When his opponents gathered around him and asked awkward questions, Stephen answered them. When they were critical, he dealt with their criticisms. If they wanted to know something, he told them. But it wasn't only what he said that was impressive. It was the way he said it. There was something so compelling and dynamic about his words that, according to Scripture, even his bitterest foes couldn't "stand up against his wisdom or the Spirit by whom he spoke" (Acts 6:10).

As we have already seen, the defeated man has trouble with his talking as well as his walking. But when Stephen spoke, he did so with power and authority. This is the kind of talking that people in the world appreciate. They are sick of mealy-mouthed ministers and double-talking politicians. They want something definite, something that rings true. They got it from Stephen in his day, and they deserve it from us in our day. I have discovered that, contrary to many opinions, those who don't know the Lord often welcome straight talk and despise evasive talking. So many people are so unsure of themselves that they respect those who know what they believe and can explain why they believe it.

There is nothing to fear if you have something positive to say and you say it positively. But there is much about which to be apprehensive if you have a message you cannot or will not divulge. God will hold you responsible.

Please do not misunderstand me on this point. I am not suggesting for one moment that everyone will get in a line to kiss you when you speak like Stephen. Some of them, like Stephen's congregation, will rise up to kill you, or at least harm you. Yes, some will respond, and the rest will react, but there will be no apathy if you speak as Stephen spoke.

The secret of his speaking wasn't his homiletic ability or his oratorical polish. He was a businessman who preached in his spare time. He was a pen-pusher to earn his living and a witness to fulfill his vocation. Stephen didn't say any old thing that came into his head. There was tremendous wisdom in his speaking. This is obvious if you read through the talk he gave to the men who subsequently killed him.

It was an absolute masterpiece. He didn't have time to prepare it, either. He was thrust into a situation where he had to speak right off the cuff, and what a great job he did. His talk was full of the Old Testament. He gave a brilliant exposition of the history of his people. There is no doubt about it—he knew his Bible.

This is part of the problem today. Pew-sitters don't know their Bibles as they ought. You will never speak with authority if you don't tell people what God says in language they understand. And you will never be able to do this if you don't know your Bible.

There is no short-cut to knowing the Word of God. There are no twentieth-century methods of instant Bible knowledge. We have instant coffee, instant banking, and instant information. These are all devised to save time and energy, but there will never be an instant Bible-study method. Get your nose into the Book like Stephen did, or you will never have anything irresistible to say!

This may sound as if he gave a first-class sermon. I've no doubt that he did, but it all depends on what you mean by a sermon. I have heard sermons that were excellent in wisdom and outline, and they put everyone to sleep. I have heard testimonies that were honest and sincere but as flat as pancakes. There was something about Stephen's words, however, that we must not miss. It was the *spirit* in which he spoke as well as the wisdom with which he spoke that made his words irresistible. There was a contagious enthusiasm and spontaneity that must have been a thrill to behold, judging from the thrill we get from just reading it!

Dangerous people believe what they believe so much that it shows on their faces. Their convictions are so real and their messages are delivered in such fresh, lively, natural tones that the listeners are caught up in the sheer exuberance of the message.

No doubt you have heard people speak with great wisdom and little spirit. On the other hand, maybe you have met some full of spirit and sadly lacking in wisdom. The former speaker puts his listeners to sleep, while the latter annoys his listeners beyond words. Both are ineffective. Wisdom and spirit need to be married if our words are to be irresistible.

Stephen was a great man. His life didn't take him to the top of any popularity poll on earth, but the Lord Jesus himself stood to welcome him as he made his way to heaven. Who cares about fickle popularity polls when the acclamation of heaven is a possibility? Better to live briefly and dangerously for God than to live a long and easy life for yourself. It is infinitely richer to be God's person on earth seeing God at work, making inroads into enemy territory, than to be saved but defeated.

When and how should a Christian be dangerous today? Charles Colson provides one example. But you don't have to change the basic arrangement of your life and enter "full-time ministry." Stephen didn't. On your job and in your neighborhood there are people who need the witness of a loving, dangerous Christian. In your city, there are hurting people who need for dangerous Christians to stick out their necks and their helping hands. Your city also has people in league with Satan, such as pornographers, who ought to be confronted lovingly but firmly by dangerous men and women of God. And if your church has grown cold and ineffective, it needs the active presence of dangerous believers.

Where is God calling *you* to be involved as one of his dangerous people?

Let's Get Practical

1. How can "everyday Christians" make a positive impact on the world?

2. What are three ways Stephen's life is an example to us?

3. What are some of the things you could see a person like Stephen doing today in our churches and communities?

4. What can "the people in the pew" do to help solve the problem of getting God's message to the people who need to hear it?

5. How does thinking about Stephen's character, actions, and words challenge you personally? What is one area of your life in which you would like to become more like him?

10

The Indispensable Person

Acts 6

Many books today promise you the "secret keys" to one sort of success or another. Well, we Christians should all hunger for the kind of spiritual effectiveness that Stephen had back at the birth of the church and that a man like Charles Colson experiences now. Certainly Joe (about whom I told you at the beginning of chapter 9) and the rest of us who are like him to one degree or another need to learn to employ their spiritual secret.

But Stephen's and Colson's key to effectiveness is really no secret at all. If you read again the biblical account of Stephen, looking particularly for the root of his power, it becomes clear when you notice a certain phrase that is repeated more than once in connection with his name. I am certain that the Spirit of God led Doctor Luke to repeat himself in order that we might have no possible chance of missing it.

In Acts 6:5, Stephen is described as "a man full of faith and of the Holy Spirit"; then, in verse 8, as "full of God's grace and power." It is also important to see what kind of man the apostles required to look after the business: "full of the Spirit and of wisdom" (v. 3). Do you see the word *full* recurring?

Everyone is full of something. Some are full of themselves. They are so impressed with themselves that they are almost unbearable. People find them extremely tiresome and *un*impressive. You have probably met people who are full of problems, or perhaps the kind of people who appear to be happy only when they are miserable. Some have a consuming ambition and are full of plans and ideas revolving around themselves.

The Secret of Effective People

Stephen was likewise full of something. He was full of the Spirit and wisdom—full of faith and of the Holy Spirit—full of God's grace and power. Whatever fills a person drives a person, and whatever drives a person determines what he is, what he does, and what he says.

One thing the apostles said always shakes me. When they were looking for church administration, they insisted first of all that anyone who was not filled with the Holy Spirit need not apply. In those days, suitability for administrative posts in the church was determined by spiritual condition.

Is that the case today? I fear not. Often the people who are responsible for the spiritual leadership (let alone the administrators) of the church are not even examined on this point. When you think about it, it isn't really surprising that we are losing our grip. It isn't hard to see the falling away of standards since those early, dynamic days.

How can we possibly hope to make an impact on our day and age when we neglect the basic considerations of God's requirements? We are more concerned about education than spirituality. Popular preaching is more in demand than deep exposition of the Word of God. The people we elect to run the affairs of our churches are chosen for their business ability more than their spiritual integrity.

By all means, let us have business people for business positions in the church, and give us educated people for educated congregations, but don't let us mistake natural ability for spiritual dynamic.

Filled with the Holy Spirit first, highly qualified second—that is the correct order.

There are reasons for the reluctance of the twentieth-century church to think in terms of the fullness of the Holy Spirit. One reason is suspicion. "I've heard about the funny things that happen when these folks get all filled, and I said to my husband, I'm having nothing to do with it!" Another is ignorance. "I can't understand the differences between the Holy Spirit working and Jesus living in my heart. I get so confused that I have decided to leave it alone." Or believe it or not, denominational differences enter into the subject. "I'm an Episcopalian, and I don't want to have anything to do with this Pentecostalism!"

It must be said in no uncertain terms that there have been abuses and excesses in the name of the Holy Spirit. There are those who are misleading the children of God on this subject. But any child of God who says, "I am not getting involved in this doctrine of the Holy Spirit" is really saying, "I'm not going to get involved in God's kind of Christianity." It is as serious as that, for *it is impossible for a child of God to live triumphantly and effectively in this day and age unless he does so under the dominion of the Lord and through the fullness of his Spirit.*

Receive the Holy Spirit

I do not propose at this juncture to dive into any argument on this vital subject. Suffice to say that there is nothing to be afraid of concerning the fullness of the Spirit, save missing it! Instead, I prefer to outline very briefly what is involved.

The first step to enjoying the fullness of the Spirit is to realize that you received him when you were converted. When you talk about receiving Christ, you are saying the same thing as receiving the Holy Spirit. It is obvious that you could not possibly have received Christ physically into your body, so the only possibility is that you received him spiritually. The only way the Lord acts in a spiritual capacity is through his Spirit—the Holy Spirit. Therefore, to receive Christ spiritually, you invite the risen Lord to come into your life through the Holy Spirit.

Be filled with the Holy Spirit

The next step is to realize that it is possible to receive the Holy Spirit but not to be filled with the Holy Spirit. The Christians at Ephesus, who became Christians the same way that anyone becomes a Christian, by receiving Christ, were told to be filled with the Spirit whom they had already received. The reception of the Holy Spirit and the fullness of the Holy Spirit are not synonymous.

Realize it's a command

The third step is to note that Christians are commanded to be filled. This is not an optional extra for those who want "to go in for this sort of thing." It is a categorical requirement of God for his people if they are to live a life of effectiveness.

Realize who the Holy Spirit is

The fourth step is at first sight an elementary one, but nonetheless important. It is to realize who the Holy Spirit is. There is an appalling ignorance among Christians concerning the Holy Spirit. A few days ago, a young Christian told me she had discovered that the Holy Spirit was a person! But what kind of person, she still hadn't discovered. Let me give you a golden rule concerning him that will help you appreciate what kind of person the Holy Spirit really is: Whenever God does anything big, he does it through his Holy Spirit.

In creation. In the first chapter of the Bible is an account of something really big. God is creating the universe. The second verse states, "and the Spirit of God was hovering over the waters." It is obvious that more than meaningless movement is meant here. The Spirit of God in some tremendous way was responsible for the mighty movements that were involved in the mighty work of creation. He was part of the dynamic of creation—that mighty force that is beyond our understanding. He is big, he thinks big, and he moves big.

In the Incarnation. Then move on to another mighty happening in this world's history, the Incarnation. This is the event that brought the eternal Son of God to the womb of a virgin. When the girl Mary was told what was going to happen, she apparently remained remarkably composed: "How will this be, since I am a virgin?" (Luke 1:34).

Now, bearing in mind the golden rule, we know the answer in advance. Listen to this: "The Holy Spirit will come upon you" (Luke 1:35). Of course! How else would God work? For whenever he does anything big like Creation or Incarnation, he does it through the Holy Spirit.

In the Temptation. Move on to another mighty event, the temptation of the Lord Jesus in the wilderness. You know the story, but have you noticed that important detail? "Jesus, full of the Holy Spirit . . . was led by the Spirit in the desert" (Luke 4:1). He went into that mighty conflict with evil personified, in the power of the Spirit. Then he came out of the desert, and note carefully what the Scripture states: "Jesus returned . . . in the power of the Spirit" (Luke 4:14).

Now, if the Holy Spirit was so eager for us to know the condition of the Lord when he went in and when he came out, it would appear perfectly obvious that he wanted us to know that his condition was unchanged all through the shattering experience. He was filled with the Spirit. The dynamic of God in his life that enabled him as a man to overthrow the might of Satan was the Holy Spirit.

In the Crucifixion. Turn in your thoughts to the next mighty event of this world's history, the crucifixion of Jesus Christ. Did you ever wonder where the Lord Jesus got the power to endure the physical agony and the spiritual suffering that he went through? Have you ever tried to think what it was that enabled him *to be made sin,* and to willingly offer himself as a sacrifice to God for sin?

It was a chilling time, full of cruel passion and bitter hatred. He faced the rejection of his people, the desertion of his friends, the estrangement of his Father, and the taunts of the crowd. Suffering and sin mingled with shame and spitting to make this event the all-time low of human behavior.

Those hours on the cross were the very habitation of human iniquity, and in the midst of it hung Jesus. How did he bear it? Listen! "Christ . . . through the eternal Spirit offered himself unblemished to God" (Heb. 9:14). The Spirit of God was the enabling force even on that "wondrous cross."

In the Resurrection. But Jesus did not stay dead. On the third day he rose again—triumphant and glorious. He wasn't surprised to find himself back on earth. He had been saying repeatedly that he would be back. His disciples didn't believe him, but his enemies had their suspicions!

Think hard for a moment. Jesus was dead. His body lay in the tomb. The stone was at the entrance. The guard stood nearby. Jesus was in the realm of Paradise. He had been made sin, and he had sunk under the awful wrath of God. Defeat for the crucified appeared a foregone conclusion. Then suddenly the stone rolled away, the grave clothes rolled aside, the guards fell to the ground, and the mighty Son of God moved in irresistible power once again. Raised from the dead! How did he do it? "If the Spirit of him who raised Jesus from the dead . . ." (Rom. 8:11). He, the Spirit of God, was in action on that mighty day, as he always has been in action when anything big is being done.

There is so much more to be said about who the Holy Spirit is, but if we can only grasp the immensity of his person and the possibilities of his fullness, that will suffice for now. Have you seen that when you invited Christ to come into your life, he did it in the person of the Holy Spirit, who is always in business when God is doing something big?

Expect the Holy Spirit to Invade Your Life

The actual meaning of fullness needs to be clarified. Many people seem to think the Holy Spirit behaves rather like a liquid. The word *fullness* or the expression *filled* has understandably given rise to this mistake. You may even have heard that before a person can be filled with the Spirit, he must be emptied of self. It is in the same way that a cup full of water can only be filled with milk after the cup has been emptied. However, this is a slightly misleading analogy.

The Bible teaches that you will never be emptied of self. Your old, sinful nature is with you for the rest of your days on earth. So if you are wanting to be emptied of self, you are wanting something the Bible says you won't get. Further, if you feel you can never be filled with the Spirit until you have banished self, you will have a long wait. Scripture teaches that the Spirit will wage a continuous battle against the sinful nature within you. It is obvious, therefore, that self will continue to be in evidence.

Don't get too excited, for this does not mean that you can indulge in self and be filled with the Spirit at the same time. Not at all! To be filled with the Spirit means that the self is overpowered by the indwelling dynamic of the Spirit of God.

Remember that the Bible draws a parallel between being drunk and being filled with the Spirit. You may be like me in that you have never been drunk, but you don't have to be drunk to know something about it. It is not necessary to be emptied of everything with a stomach pump in order to be filled with wine and therefore drunk. In my case, I would need very little to make me drunk. All I would need would be enough wine to overpower my faculties, and I would be drunk.

This is the meaning of the fullness of the Spirit. It is his overpowering. People are filled with the Spirit when they are prepared to abandon themselves to his dominion and rejoice in this overpowering.

We must claim the Holy Spirit's power and enabling and expect him to move in and through our lives. It is not uncommon to have a firm belief in the theoretical possibilities of the Lord's working in your life without having any sense of anticipation that he will do so. Now we must underline the necessity of claiming the full empowering of the Spirit and *expecting* him to start work through our lives.

Much has been written and said about the evidences of the fullness of the Spirit. There are those who believe that the only true evidence of this fullness is speaking in tongues and other such signs. This, I believe, is not true, and I further believe that it can lead to great difficulties. On the other hand, there are those who hold an untenable position by stating that there is no such thing as speaking in tongues in this dispensation. My own conviction is that the unfailing evidence of the dynamic of the Spirit of God must be demonstrated, not so much by supernatural signs, but by the fruit of the Spirit. In certain instances it may also be seen in the gifts of the Spirit. Signs are no substitute for fruit, but they may be an addition to fruit. Therefore, major on the fruit and not the gifts. Get them in perspective, and the Spirit of God himself will protect you from abuse and excess.

There is no evidence that Stephen spoke in tongues, but there is great evidence that the Spirit of God got a wonderful grip on Stephen's tongue. It is quite possible that Stephen's miracles included healings, but there is no need to spend time surmising when there is so much evidence of the fruit of the Spirit in his life.

The analogy of the drunken man helps here. A drunken man doesn't need to go around announcing that he is drunk. If he is drunk, it will be obvious.

I went to a wedding one day where a little man got drunk. He staggered in my direction with the greatest difficulty. As he drew level with me, he lurched at an alarming angle. Then to my amazement he said to me, "I know what you're trying to do. You're trying to trip me up." He spoke with the thick, slurred voice of a drunken man so that I had difficulty understanding what he was saying.

Finally, when I heard him properly, I assured him that I had no intention of tripping him up, and that in his condition, if I breathed on him it would have been all that was required to put him on the floor.

To my intense embarrassment, he peeled off his jacket and, swaying in the breeze, adopted a stance that would have done credit to Muhammad Ali. He was really in a bad state. But notice that his drunken condition affected him three ways—the way he walked, the way he talked, and the way he thought. A man filled with the Spirit demonstrates the same symptoms.

Stephen certainly did. His walk was so exemplary that everyone knew he belonged to the Lord. His talking was so affected that his words were winged home in the power of the Spirit, and who can dispute the fact that his thinking was governed by the Spirit! When they murdered him, he died praying that the Lord would forgive his murderers!

Don't be afraid of being filled with the Spirit. Settle for nothing less than his mighty invasion of your whole being. He is your only hope. He is the secret of all spiritual effectiveness. Only when the Lord, who died for you and rose again to live in you, is allowed to rule over you through his Spirit will you know what it is to be dangerous to the devil.

If you desire his fullness, say this prayer sincerely:

Dear Lord, now I am beginning to understand who the Holy Spirit is. I realize he is in me and he wants to overpower me. This is what I want, too. I now submit to your lordship and claim his fullness by faith. Thank you for what you will do through me for Jesus' sake. Amen.

Let's Get Practical

1. What is the one essential key to an effective Christian life?

2. What were the requirements for leadership in the New Testament church? How do they compare with the requirements for leaders in the church today?

3. What does it mean to be full of the Holy Spirit?

4. What is the best gauge of how "full" we are of the Holy Spirit?

5. As you reflect on the past week, what would your actions and words suggest that you are "full of"? What seems to be the main controlling factor in your life?

11

Winners Never Quit

Never make the mistake of thinking that the fullness of the Holy Spirit is one blinding experience that sees you through the rest of your days. Almost invariably, Christians come to an understanding and experience of abandoning themselves to his dynamic control through a crisis, but that is only the beginning. Crises develop into processes.

C. S. Lewis offers an eloquent analogy that speaks of the ongoing, sometimes difficult process of allowing the Holy Spirit to control our lives:

Imagine yourself as a living house. God [in the Person of the Spirit] comes in to rebuild that house. At first, perhaps, you can understand what he is doing. He is getting the drains right and stopping the leaks in the roof and so on: you knew that those jobs needed doing and so you are not surprised. But presently he starts knocking the house about in a way that hurts abominably and does not seem to make sense. What on earth is he up to? The explanation is that he is building quite a different house from the one you thought of—throwing out a new wing here, putting on an extra floor there, running up towers, making courtyards. You thought you were going to be made into a decent little cottage: but he is building a palace. He intends to come and live in it himself.[1]

This continual growth in yieldedness to the control of the Holy Spirit is what it means to be filled with the Spirit daily. When Stephen was chosen by the Christians to be a deacon, he was full of the Holy Spirit. Previously they had been looking for that kind of man, and they knew that he had been filled with the Spirit. When he was murdered, he looked steadfastly heavenward as the stones shattered his body, and he was full of the Holy Spirit.

Full of the Holy Spirit

It is significant that the Scriptures are so careful to describe the condition of Stephen over a period of time. There is a serious misconception about the fullness of the Spirit. Many people seem to have gained the impression that the fullness of the Spirit is obtained in a blinding, exhilarating, supernatural experience so overwhelmingly dynamic that the recipient is never the same again.

This was not the case in Stephen's experience. No doubt he did have an initial experience when he intelligently, willingly abandoned himself body, soul, and spirit to the Christ who through the Holy Spirit had taken up residence deep in the recesses of his being. Without question, this experience would have far-reaching consequences.

But there was more involved than a single experience. There had to be a continual, step-by-step consciousness of the sufficiency and the all-powerful presence of the indwelling Spirit. More than that, there had to be a continual acknowledging of his sovereign lordship and an unswerving dependence and reliance upon him to control, fill, and flood his being. It was as necessary for Stephen to enjoy the fullness of the Spirit when he sat at his desk as when he worked his wonders.

---

1. C. S. Lewis, *Mere Christianity* (New York: MacMillan, 1960), P. 174.

Stephen's remarkable composure and victory at the moment of his decease was the direct result of his abandonment to the Spirit of God. But Stephen didn't need to be filled with the Spirit only to die a martyr's death; he also had to be filled with the Spirit in order to live a Christian life. It is the continual fullness of the Spirit that is so important and so often tragically disregarded.

The old, sinful nature was still very much alive in Stephen, although you wouldn't think so. But the only reason you wouldn't think so was that the Spirit of God was being allowed to overpower this sin principle and continually deliver Stephen from the "law of sin and death."

Even Stephen could have preached in the energy of the flesh. He could have resisted his enemies in the fury of mighty indignation at the way they were treating him. I have no doubt that Stephen had it in him even to deny the Lord with oaths and curses when he saw that his life was in jeopardy.

But he didn't, because at every moment that he knew the pressure of sin within him to react in the ways suggested above, he related this intolerable pressure to the controlling, mighty power of the Spirit of him who raised up Christ from the dead. And the Holy Spirit took over and demonstrated his mighty power through a body, soul, and spirit that we call Stephen.

The relationship between the initial filling of the life of the risen Christ through the Holy Spirit and the subsequent continual filling can be illustrated from a common human experience.

Did you ever hear of a girl falling in love? I'm sure you have. When the girl fell in love, she felt that her heart was full to overflowing, and that if she had any more love she would burst. And on the day of her marriage, she had to admit that she loved her new husband even more than she had ever loved him.

Perhaps their marriage developed along certain lines, and they encountered all kinds of hardship and disappointment. This only served to deepen her love for her husband. And when he fell seriously ill after many wonderful years of marriage, during which they had triumphed over trial and disappointment, she nursed him almost to the point of exhaustion. Never once did she complain.

Not for a moment did she object, for her love was all-powerful, prepared to go to all lengths.

If on the day of her husband's death you were to ask her, "Do you love him more now than the day you first fell in love?" I think I know what she would say. With a sad smile she would affirm, "When I first met him, I thought that if I loved him any more I would burst. But now as I look back, I can see that what I thought was a love that couldn't increase was nothing more than the beginnings of a love that has increased day by day."

The first day that a man opens his life to the Spirit of God in all his fullness, he may be forgiven for thinking that he couldn't possibly ever know more of his presence and his sufficiency. But years of experience and days of all manner of trials and opportunities, victories and defeats, will only serve to deepen his capacity, which the Spirit of God will be delighted to fill.

The dangerous man is never beyond the possibility of defeat. The Spirit-filled man will never be out of reach of the sin nature and human selfishness. There is no human being this side of eternity who can anticipate anything but conflict, for the more dangerous we become, the more attacks we can expect from the evil one.

During the war, I lived close to one of Britain's biggest ship-building yards. The largest aircraft carriers were built there, and as a teenager I enjoyed watching these massive vessels being built.

The enemy knew all about them, of course, and was intent on destroying them before they were ever put to sea. But he did a wise thing. When the ships were first started he ignored them. As time went by and the aircraft carriers came nearer and nearer to completion, he showed more and more interest. Reconnaissance aircraft began to appear with increasing regularity.

Then one night, when we were all expecting it, he came and bombed the almost completed ship. As night followed night, the attacks increased in ferocity and intensity. It developed into a race. Would the ship sail first, or would the bombs hit and sink her? The longer the men worked on the ship, the more dangerous she became. The more dangerous she became, the more violent the attack.

I am glad to say that every ship escaped fully complete and fully operative.

The more dangerous you become through ever increasing fullness, the more you can expect attack. As the attacks increase, your vulnerability will increase. But in the degree in which your vulnerability is increased, your dependence upon the Spirit must also increase. And he will not fail.

I get worried when I hear people talking in glib, unthinking, silly language about victory in the Christian life. They seem to think that victory means vacation. Victory presupposes battle, not vacation.

Of course, there is the other extreme. Some saints are so busy concentrating on the battles that they never win one through the power of the Spirit of God. The result is that they rapidly come to the conclusion that the Christian life is a battle and nothing more. On the contrary, the Christian life is a battle that you are expected to win.

There will be no victory without a battle, but there need be no battle that ends in defeat. This was Stephen's experience. He lived a day-by-day, situation-after-situation experience of the fullness that God made available to him. Is this your experience?

The fullness we have talked about leads to other things that we need to discover. Remember how we noted that Stephen was not only full of the Spirit, but also full of wisdom, faith, grace, and power. The fullness of these qualities comes as a result of the working of the indwelling Holy Spirit.

Full of Wisdom

I have no doubt that Stephen was an intelligent man. But there is more than intelligence involved in what the Bible calls wisdom. It is not uncommon to come across highly intelligent people who are seriously lacking in wisdom. On the other hand, it is always a delight to meet people who are not particularly well endowed with natural wisdom or intelligence, but who obviously have the touch of God on their lives, and who demonstrate a deep grasp of the things of God.

Stephen was very conscious of the importance of this wisdom that enables people to come to grips with all that God intends for us to know and understand. It is interesting that he mentioned two men in his survey of the history of the children of Israel who were characterized by wisdom.

He explained how God gave Joseph "favor and wisdom in the sight of Pharaoh" (Acts 7:10). Joseph lived before the heathen king in such a remarkable way that even he had to admit that there was a divine quality about the young foreigner. Joseph's grasp of the essentials and the deep convictions that governed his behavior were so impressive to Pharaoh that even though he had no time for Joseph's God, he had to acknowledge that Joseph's God was doing a good job on Joseph!

Moses was the other man who had wisdom, but it was a different type of wisdom. He was without doubt a brilliant man, greatly endowed with natural intelligence, handsome and striking in his bearing. He was highly trained and deeply versed—but in the wisdom of the Egyptians.

No doubt this wisdom sharpened his wits and equipped him for all manner of tasks. In all probability it taught him how to master the engineering difficulties inherent in building a pyramid. He probably had an advanced understanding of writing and literature.

But it certainly did nothing toward equipping him in a deeper knowledge of his God or to prepare him to deal with the spiritual problems of the people he was destined to lead.

Perhaps if Moses had enjoyed more of the wisdom of God, like Joseph, and less of the wisdom of Egypt, things might have been different. For instance, he would not have needed to ask God what his name was. He would not have refused to go where God sent him. He would have gone. He would not have bemoaned his own insufficiency but would have rejoiced in the all-sufficiency of the great I Am. He would not have said his mouth couldn't give God's message. He would have relied on his God to give him the words to speak. The wisdom of this world is a great asset, but it is no substitute for the wisdom that God gives through his Spirit.

Understanding Scripture

As I mentioned in an earlier chapter, Stephen clearly demonstrated a fine grasp of the Scriptures. The Spirit of God uses the Scriptures to impart to the child of God the wisdom of God. It is exciting to realize that the same Holy Spirit who inspired the Scriptures takes up his abode in the heart of a Christian to interpret them.

What more could a child of God desire? Every born-again believer has available to him the One who was responsible for putting into writing the unknown mysteries of God! This means that every Christian has the golden opportunity of having a personal revelation and an intimate interpretation of the truth of God at any time. But, of course, he must first be in an attitude toward the Word of God that will allow the Spirit of God to speak to his heart.

Unfortunately, there is a great dearth of spiritual insight and wisdom among Christians today because Christians will not dig into the Word for themselves.

Wisdom we need

I once gave a talk in California, encouraging young people in a Bible college to make certain that they spent time in the Word of God every day. I tried to impress upon them that reading the Bible is not necessarily studying the Word of God. Many people read the Bible regularly, but they never study the Word. Some do not have the Spirit of God to make it make sense to them. Others go through a cursory daily ritual of reading a portion, but they never benefit because they do not allow the Spirit of God to speak to them through the Word. They are too busy to be still and meditate.

After I had given the talk, a student came to me and accused me of being "unrealistic." She said, "How can you be so unrealistic as to suggest that we spend time daily in the Word of God? We live busy lives, and it is impossible to give the time that you seem to think is necessary."

I asked her if she ever ate food.

111

She replied in the affirmative.

"To feed your body?" I inquired.

She nodded.

I further asked how long she estimated that she spent daily feeding her body.

She estimated approximately one hour every day. She admitted that her body would eventually die and return to the dust from which it had come, but she insisted that she ought to continue feeding it.

But she had no answer when I asked her, "Why do you consider it unrealistic to take time to nourish your soul that will never pass away when you find it necessary to feed your body for one hour every day, knowing full well that it will inevitably pass away?"

The only unrealistic thing about spending time daily in allowing the Spirit of God to impart wisdom to your soul through the written Word of God is failing to do it! And this is exactly what men and women are doing today. As a result, they, like Moses, have a great grasp of the wisdom of the "Egyptians" and an ominous lack of the wisdom of God that Joseph and Stephen enjoyed and shared.

Wisdom the world needs

The wisdom that God gave Joseph, and which he shared with Pharaoh, affected the attitude of the Egyptian monarch. In the same way, Stephen's wisdom had a great impact on the people of his time.

People in this "enlightened" twentieth century are confused because we know how to get to the moon, but not how to get to heaven. We have discovered how to make life, but we don't know how to live our own lives. We know how to conquer space, but we still can't conquer sin.

People today desperately need a vision of what God can do in our lives and an understanding of what God has provided for our lives.

Those of us who are intended to tell the Good News fail if we are so busy with the wrong kind of wisdom that we, like Moses, have nothing of value to contribute to the thousands who would appreciate the opportunity to hear. This is the sad aspect of failing to appropriate the wisdom of God and the Spirit he longs to impart.

Full of Faith

The second quality I want you to notice is Stephen's fullness of faith. It is quite clear from the way in which Stephen is described that his fullness of faith was linked with his experience of the Holy Spirit in his life. He was "full of faith and of the Holy Spirit" (Acts 6:5).

There are few more important topics for Christians than the topic of faith. The more I study the Word of God, the more I am impressed by the fact that every aspect of the Christian life appears to operate on a principle of faith: Christian experience begins with salvation; we are saved by grace through faith (see Ephesians 2:8). Then the Christian is expected to stand fast, and we read that it is "by faith that we stand." But this does not mean that the Christian is allowed to be stationary; "we walk by faith." As Christians walk, we encounter all kinds of problems that need cause us no lasting concern, for we can overcome them through faith. When we need advice from our Lord, we can go to him through "the prayer of faith."

In fact, the whole of the Christian experience is summarized in the oft-repeated words of Scripture "The just shall live by faith." Stephen was full of faith. Every area of his life was enriched because of the quality of his faith.

It is good to be reminded that everyone is full of faith. We wake up in the morning, look at the clock, and believe. We switch on the light and expect it to work. We jump out of bed and trust the floorboards. We inhale deeply and never check what we are breathing. We stagger to the bathroom and turn on the tap, assuming it will produce water and not sulphuric acid. And so on. Never a moment of a person's life is lived on any other principle than faith. We cannot operate without reliance and dependence on things and people all the time.

But of course, Stephen's faith was much more than this everyday kind of faith. Otherwise there would have been no necessity to comment on it. It is the object of Stephen's faith that was so extraordinary. The object of faith is always the most vital factor.

Some people have strong faith in weak ice. Nothing is at fault in their faith except, of course, the object! When the object of faith is wrong, everything is wrong. We hardly need to be reminded that the object of Stephen's faith was God, who reigned supreme in heaven and at the same time, through the Holy Spirit, reigned supreme in Stephen.

He trusted his Lord with everything. Even his dying words showed glorious dependence and faith: "Lord Jesus, receive my Spirit." In the hour of greatest battle, his eyes were on heaven and his heart was at rest. In the time of his greatest agony, he saw with eyes of faith "the Son of Man standing at the right hand of God" (Acts 7:56). This faith was unshaken by attack and unmoved by circumstances. In fact, it persisted in growing stronger.

Faith in the right object always grows stronger. That is why I have some difficulty understanding people who insist on asking God for more faith. If they were convinced of the possibilities of the indwelling Lord cutting loose in their lives because they allowed him the right to cut loose, he would! And once a man has seen the Lord really cutting loose, he is much more likely to try it again at the next opportunity.

This is a common fact of life. Have you ever seen someone about to travel on a plane for the first time? He will hop from one foot to the other and chew on his lower lip while waiting to board. When the announcement to board the aircraft is given, he will dash to a seat by the emergency exit. The roar of the engines and the sickening feeling in the pit of the stomach as the plane leaves the ground will almost reduce him to hysteria.

But notice the same person six hours later. He is calm and relaxed—reading and chatting, smiling and eating. What has happened to him? Did God give him more faith? No! He started off with very little faith, which he timidly placed, with grave suspicion, in the plane. As time wore on, he realized that the plane was trustworthy. It didn't disintegrate. It didn't explode. So he relaxed a little more, then more, and still more. The more he was convinced

114

of the faithfulness of the plane, the quicker he showed a fullness of faith that did the plane justice.

A Christian who has taken the Lord at his word and seen him work is much more likely to trust him again more completely. If you have a weak faith, it is because you haven't trusted the Lord with the faith that you have. If you had trusted him, you would have found him trustworthy, and more faith would automatically have developed.

Over the time that Stephen had known the Lord, this had been his experience. Nothing was exempt from his attitude of relaxed dependence. No time of the day or night was free from this relationship. Obviously, he wasn't always conscious of this attitude, but it was so natural to him that if he had been awakened out of sleep by a crisis, faith would have been his first reaction, and the Lord would have filled his earliest thought.

There is no substitute for this kind of faith, and it can be enjoyed by all who are prepared to live by it. The will plays an important role in faith. You decide whether you will trust a person. You don't drift automatically into trust. In all probability, you satisfy yourself that the person is worthy of trust before you trust him or her.

The *will* decides whether you trust on the basis of the information that the intellect has amassed. Faith is not a nebulous, indefinable entity. Faith is an intelligent act and attitude of the will that leads a person to trust and depend upon something or someone at a given moment.

If you have difficulties in this area, check on your understanding of who the Lord is and what he promises to do, and then find out if you are prepared to let him do it. He will make of you a Stephen— full of the Holy Spirit, full of wisdom, and full of faith.

Let's Get Practical

1. Why do we need to be filled with the Holy Spirit in order to live a Christian life?

2. What is one practical way we can grow daily in God's kind of wisdom?

3. What is it about our culture and the world we live in that makes it seem so difficult to be "full" of faith in God?

4. What difficulties do you have, personally, in the area of absolute trust in God, gaining his kind of wisdom, or being constantly filled with his Holy Spirit?

5. What are three steps that you will take this week to investigate who the Holy Spirit is and how he can meet your particular need?

12

The Transformed Life Is the Powerful Life

Just a few short decades ago, Jim Elliot and three fellow missionaries, dangerous men all, went to Ecuador to present the gospel to the Auca Indians, a hostile tribe that had never heard the Good News of Jesus Christ. These men were soldiers on the front line of the battle against Satan and his forces.

Like Stephen in the New Testament, Elliot and his friends gave their lives in the cause, victims of a massacre by frightened Auca warriors who didn't understand why the white men had come. But their deaths were not in vain. God used them to open the doors to the hearts of all the Aucas, and in just a few years the entire tribe was won to Christ—including every one of the killers.

In the days of the early church, men like Stephen were also frontline soldiers of Jesus Christ. Through them, mighty victories were won, and much enemy territory was captured. Hearts that sin had held captive were flooded with light. People who had been "held captive by [the devil] to do his will" (2 Tim. 2:26) were set free from his tyranny. Even a "great many of the priests were becoming obedient to the faith" (Acts 6:7). Day after day the church moved like a mighty army, crushing opposition, throwing down strongholds. Those were thrilling and adventurous days.

They were also costly days. No wonder the forces who were suffering such major defeat began to hit back as hard as they could. The religious leaders were the first to react. They saw men who had gone along with their dead religion for years suddenly come to life. To their great dismay, they saw men and women from their synagogues moving, in ever increasing numbers, into the Christians' camp.

So great was their anger that they resorted to all kinds of illegal practices. They stirred up riots. Even the law courts were abused by them. Men were bribed to give false evidence. Lies and blasphemies increased, and anger and terror slowly and irresistibly began to rise. Then it overflowed, and the church began to learn how much people hated the gospel—Christians began to taste the sufferings of Christ.

Those early Christians were introduced to the shocking reality of real persecution. Jesus' words about "taking up the cross" and "Blessed are those who have been persecuted for the sake of righteousness" (Matt. 5:10) took on new meaning. When he said that he was sending them forth "as sheep in the midst of wolves" (Matt. 10:16), he had been giving them a painfully accurate picture of what they could expect.

No exhilarating hymns were needed to instill courage into those people. It was not necessary to use any noble catch phrases to get them moving. The battle was on, and those who belonged to the Lord were in up to their necks.

It is awe-inspiring to be confronted with all the fury of the forces of Satan fighting for survival. Strong people can be broken easily when the mighty forces of evil are aimed at them. But Stephen, in the front line, never wavered. He stood firm under the most intense pressure. He recognized the subtle attacks of the evil one, remembering that the devil does not only use his crushing strength, but that on occasion he can be subtle and disarming.

I'm not sure when Satan is most lethal. You remember when Joseph was attacked through the bitter, brutal behavior of his appalling brothers. There was an animal force about their attack that was not difficult to recognize. The devil followed up this crushing attack of brute force with the subtle, soft, disarming suggestions of a beautiful and wicked woman.

Not a person alive is equal to the attacks of Satan, for this fallen angel of light is superior in power and intelligence to the most superior person. He has at his disposal mighty armies of fallen beings, and under his rule live thousands of men and women ready to be mobilized at his command. What chance did Stephen have of surviving this sort of opposition? How could God possibly allow his child to be exposed to an enemy far his superior?

In the same way that there isn't a person equal to the might of Satan, there isn't a satanic power or personality equal to the dynamic power of the risen Christ. And the same risen Christ who by his Spirit and in all his overcoming power lived in Stephen, lives in *you.* Stephen had all he needed to stand against all that was thrown at him, simply because he had all that the Lord *is* living within him.

Do you remember when Paul told Timothy that he needed to be "strong in the grace that is in Christ Jesus" (2 Tim. 2:1)? Never assume that the only people who are strong in battle are those who were born strong. If Timothy had been naturally strong, there would have been no point in telling him to be strong. The command to be strong came to Timothy and to Stephen because in themselves they were not strong. They were told to be "strong in the grace that is in Christ Jesus!"

Full of Grace

As you remember, Stephen was "full of grace." He was simply an ordinary man who was full of the commodity that Christians are told to be full of, and which they are expected to appropriate—the grace that is in Christ Jesus.

His grace is his goodness, his attitude toward us that makes him so loving and kind, so overwhelmingly forgiving and benevolent.

It is only because of his grace that we live, move, and have our being. If his grace did not exist, we could never have known his peace. Only through grace do we receive salvation and forgiveness, eternal life and assurance. Grace is at the core of all God's dealings with humanity. For, as we have already seen, all that we deserve is God's disapproval. But the grace of God makes him reach out to us with blessing upon blessing.

However, there is another special significance in this term. For grace is not only the attitude that makes God give. It is also the blessing that God gives as a result of his attitude. In other words, the grace of God in Christ Jesus means all the things that are made available to the person who is born again.

The Bible has much to say on this subject, but there is one verse that summarizes the grace of God: "God is able to make all grace abound to you, that always having all sufficiency in everything, you may have an abundance for every good deed" (2 Cor. 9:8, KJV). Isn't that a thrilling statement? Stephen believed it!—and as a result, he was full of all that God makes available to his children through the indwelling Lord at any moment, under any circumstances. This is the ultimate adventure of the Christian life!

I am sure that Stephen needed far more patience than he naturally possessed; but through the provision of the Life within him, he was able to have plenty of patience.

No doubt the things that were said about him by those professional liars who were bribed to testify against him hurt him deeply. He may have been tempted to strike back, but he knew a power of forgiveness within him that wasn't his at all. It was the work of the Spirit of God making the life of Christ real within him.

Stephen was full of grace, not his own, but the grace that is in Christ Jesus. Therefore, Stephen could count on all that God had given him in Christ and use it. The patience and forgiving Spirit of Christ were his, so he used them. Full of grace means full of all it takes to counter all the devil throws our way.

Imagine a soldier in the midst of a great battle. As the battle progresses, his supplies of ammunition begin to run low. Then his colleague is wounded, and all his first-aid equipment has been used. At this critical moment, the enemy stages a mighty offensive and it appears that all is lost. But at the crucial hour, reinforcements arrive. Ammunition and medical help come through. Supplies never run low again. There never is a moment when there is something he needs in any of the thousands of situations that warfare brings, for he has, in vast quantities, all that he needs. Stephen, "full of grace," was that soldier.

Stephen had all the resources of his base camp, heaven, within him. He was a frontline soldier with the backing of an unbeatable army. He was full of grace, and as a result the mighty forces of evil were unable to overcome him.

Of course, it is one thing to have the grace available and another to be full of it. There are soldiers who hold an impregnable position, have all the ammunition and weapons they can use, and yet they do not win a battle.

Many wars between the Israelis and the Arabs have illustrated this graphically. With numbers and resources on their side, the Arabs were comprehensively routed by smaller forces. Why? Mainly because they did not have the will to use what they had and enjoy the victory that was theirs for the winning.

There are Christians who are in a similar lamentable position. They appear to be totally incapable of winning a victory, even though they have within them the One who has already defeated their enemy. All because they fail to count on his sufficiency. They don't have the will to win.

When the pressure builds up, they are beaten because they do not say, "Lord, because you are all I need, I will not yield. Through all that you are, I will claim the victory." This does not mean that the battle will be evaded; it means that the battle will be won. And there is all the difference in the world between the two.

Stephen did not get himself rescued from the hands of the howling mob on a magic carpet. He was left to the mercy of the gang. The battle raged on. But there is no doubt that he won that awful battle.

This dangerous man was not only a specialist in defense; he was very much an offensive soldier, too. God's grace was his defense, but the fullness of God's power was his offense. Stephen was not only "full of grace"—he was also "full of power."

Full of Power

The church today needs unlimited power if we are ever to make inroads into the vast areas of enemy territory. No pious clichés or orderly, well-organized services are going to make an impact on dens of iniquity. Lovely services and beautiful music will fail to sweep demon-possessed men and women into the kingdom. Multitudes, like those added to the church in Stephen's day, will not be added to the church by honest endeavor and ordinary procedure. More than this is needed.

It will take superhuman power to achieve anything, and the sooner we admit it, the better for all concerned.

One time a group of us decided that a large construction that had stood on the grounds of Capernwray Hall since the war ought to be removed. But it was made of solid concrete. Picks, hammers, and chisels would make no impression. Honest sweat and bulging muscles were useless. The concrete could resist every attack upon it—except one—dynamite!

There is something virile about the words *dynamite* and *dynamic*. The very sound of the words suggests action, movement, and irresistible power. *Dunamis* is the Greek word from which these words derive, and in the New Testament *dunamis* is translated "power." This is what filled Stephen. He had a dynamic charge of *dunamis* in him. He was full of power. Stephen had what it took to crack solid resistance and blow it sky high. Make no mistake; it will take this kind of explosive to get the hard core of evil splintered with the gospel in these days.

You may have been surprised to hear that we used dynamite to move our concrete slab. However, we obtained the necessary permission first. There was nothing illegal about our actions, for we were fully authorized to act in that way.

The only people who are allowed to use dynamite in this country are those who have received the authority required, for dynamite in the wrong hands is lethal. Authority and power are closely related. People who have authority without power make themselves objects of derision.

One day I saw a young policeman, full of authority and oozing with self-importance, try to arrest a large drunken man. The drunken man was too strong for him and without any effort at all deposited the young policeman in the gutter—authority and all.

An older policeman came to his rescue. There was a calm authority about him that was a joy to behold, but there was power, too. With a swift twist of his hips and a grip like iron, he whipped the legs of the drunken man from under him. Then he pulled his jacket over his head, fastening his arms round his neck, and without a word, dragged him like a sack of potatoes unceremoniously to the police station.

The young policeman, looking decidedly crestfallen, followed at a respectful distance.

The two officers of the law had equal authority, but one had the power to match his authority, and the other had none.

The Lord also said, "All authority has been given to me in heaven and on earth" (Matt. 28:18). Then he said that he would be with them. If all authority is his and he is with his people, they have all his authority—authority that is valid in heaven and on earth.

Think for a moment. Stephen had the authority of heaven behind him because the Lord was with him, but he also had the dynamic of heaven upon him because the Spirit of God was within him. Remember that the Lord added, "You shall receive power when the Holy Spirit has come upon you" (Acts 1:8).

This is the position of strength for a Christian. We have the authority of heaven behind us and the dynamic of heaven within us. Stephen believed this and as a result was full of power.

When we recognize our rightful authority, we are confident and don't have to go around trying to prove ourselves. Our authority is obvious. If we have the corresponding power, we are a force to be reckoned with. That was what made Stephen dangerous. Satan recognized his authority and hated it. He also felt the mighty impact of his power and resented it. That resulted in Stephen's being a number-one target.

Dangerous Christians don't only create danger; they attract it. The crack marksman on the field of battle will always be a prime target for the enemy. The star athlete on the football field always draws the heaviest tackling. The Christian who, like Stephen, rejoices in the all-sufficient power of the Spirit of God within draws the biggest temptations and the greatest opposition. That is why some Christians don't want to be dangerous, and they turn down the opportunity for God's kind of adventure. They prefer to be comfortable.

We live in exciting days. There is much to be done, great victories to be won. Will you settle for anything other than the fullness of the grace of God in your life that will make you able to handle all that comes your way? Are you interested in anything less than the dynamic of the Spirit of God in your life that will give the evil one plenty of headaches?

You have the authority of heaven behind you, the Spirit of God within you, and the plan of God before you. Released with all this power and authority, you will be dangerous to the enemy, for God plans to deal him a body blow through you. The Lord intends to win victories through you. Are you content to live the daily grind, never a victor, never dangerous? Or can you, will you settle for anything less than this kind of high adventure?

Let's Get Practical

1. What two aspects of grace are especially meaningful to those who are seeking to live "dangerous" Christian lives?

2. What is the source of a Christian's authority? How can we make use of the awesome power that the Lord has made available to us through his Spirit?

3. When have you observed an effective combination of power and authority? By God's grace, what do you think would happen if you were to regularly see such a combination in your local church?

4. Why is it difficult to speak the truth in love, to confront evil, to risk losing the favor of others because Christ calls us to stand on the front lines for him?

5. What is "adventurous" about a life that is so "dangerous"? How can you better participate in God's adventures in your community, in your church, and in your home?